3D PRINTING and MAKER LAB for KIDS

CREATE AMAZING PROJECTS WITH CAD DESIGN AND STEAM IDEAS

ELDRID SEQUEIRA

QUARRY

Quarto.com

© 2020 Quarto Publishing Group USA Inc.
Text © 2020 Eldrid Sequeira
Photography © 2020 Quarto Publishing Group USA Inc.

First Published in 2020 by Quarry Books, an imprint of The Quarto Group,
100 Cummings Center, Suite 265-D, Beverly, MA 01915, USA.
T (978) 282-9590 F (978) 283-2742

Quarry Books titles are also available at discount for retail, wholesale,
promotional, and bulk purchase. For details, contact the Special Sales
Manager by email at specialsales@quarto.com or by mail at The Quarto
Group, Attn: Special Sales Manager, 100 Cummings Center, Suite 265-D,
Beverly, MA 01915, USA.

ISBN: 978-1-63159-799-2

Digital edition published in 2020
eISBN: 978-1-63159-800-5

Library of Congress Cataloging-in-Publication Data

Names: Sequeira, Eldrid, author.
Title: 3D printing and maker lab for kids : create amazing projects with
  CAD design and STEAM ideas / Eldrid Sequeira.
Description: Beverly, MA : Quarry Books, an imprint of The Quarto Group,
  2020. | Series: Lab for kids | Audience: Ages 8-13. |
  Audience: Grades 4-6. | Summary: "3D printing and maker lab for kids
  presents hands-on activities for learning how to use browser-based
  software TinkerCAD and SketchUp to design and print projects, along with
  informative sidebars to support related STEAM concepts"-- Provided by
  publisher.
Identifiers: LCCN 2019041105 (print) | LCCN 2019041106 (ebook) | ISBN
  9781631597992 (paperback) | ISBN 9781631598005 (ebook)
Subjects: LCSH: Three-dimensional printing--Juvenile literature. |
  Makerspaces--Juvenile literature.
Classification: LCC TS171.95 .S46 2020 (print) | LCC TS171.95 (ebook) |
  DDC 621.9/88--dc23
LC record available at https://lccn.loc.gov/2019041105
LC ebook record available at https://lccn.loc.gov/2019041106

Design and Page Layout: Kathie Alexander
Cover Images: Glenn Scott Photography
Photography: Glenn Scott Photography, except by Shutterstock on pages 8
and 116, and by Eldrid Sequeira on page 63.

DEDICATION

TO MY FATHER
WHO FOSTERED MY DESIRE TO THINK

CONTENTS

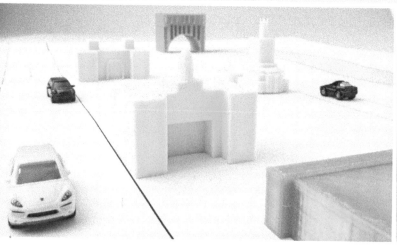
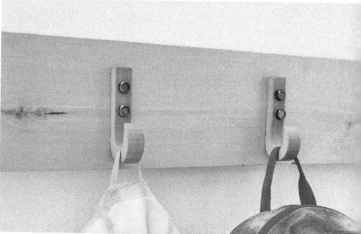

Introduction: Welcome to CAD Design & 3D Printing! 6
3D Printing Basics 8

MAKING 3D PROJECTS WITH TINKERCAD

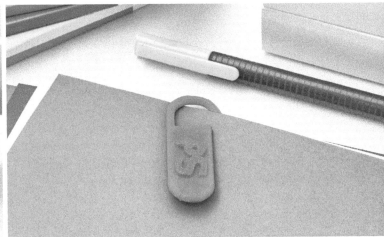

MAKING 3D PROJECTS
WITH SKETCHUP

INTRODUCTION

WELCOME TO CAD DESIGN & 3D PRINTING!

In *3D Printing and Maker Lab for Kids*, we look at the process of designing physical objects through the concept of *material manipulation*.

Many objects are made from raw materials that are usually available in fixed shapes and sizes—for example, rolls of metal, sheets of paper, bars of iron, and so on—and we can create the objects we want by manipulating these raw materials. This includes combining different shapes, changing their sizes, breaking them apart, partially joining them, and attaching two or more different materials. Typically, these actions require an intermediate step: gluing to combine, sawing to break something up, or hinging to make a flexible connection. By contrast, in the world of Computer-Aided Design—usually called CAD—these kinds of steps can be eliminated. In this book, we take a look at each of these processes and build a variety of objects that explain how they work in CAD.

3D Printing and Maker Lab for Kids also shows how to create designs in two different CAD programs: Tinkercad and SketchUp. Both applications are free; all you need is an Internet connection and a web browser to access them. And while both are fairly easy for beginners to learn, we use Tinkercad to make most of the projects because it has a shorter learning curve. The remaining projects are made in SketchUp, which unlike Tinkercad uses preset 2D objects that must be converted into 3D.

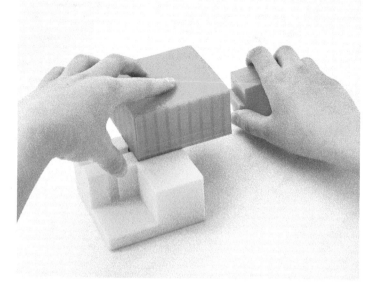

In addition to giving you the tools to develop your ability to visualize your designs through CAD, we also provide guidance on how to manufacture them through 3D printing. The ease of 3D printing offers the opportunity to revise and reprint as you explore the design and performance of each version. There are many ways to design an object; see which one works the most efficiently or is the most challenging to create or operate.

You're about to embark on a journey that will change your view of our physical world. Enjoy dreaming, designing, and making!

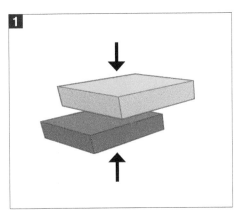

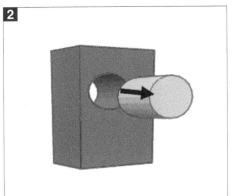

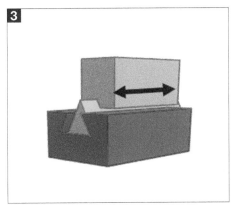

In this book, we explore how to manipulate and combine materials and elements through CAD and 3D printing in a variety of ways:

1. *Creating permanent joints and/or merging materials*

2. *Removing material (making holes or cuts)*

3. *Creating temporary joints/merging materials/limited joints*

4. *Making complex materials through a series of manipulations*

5. *Mixing different types of materials (metal, fabric, organic, etc.)*

3D PRINTING BASICS

The process of 3D printing is essentially a manufacturing technology to create objects in three dimensions (as opposed to 2D printing of documents on paper) using various materials heated to a temperature that allows them to be formed into different shapes. It has gained much popularity in the past couple of decades due to the abundance of reasonably priced desktop 3D printers available on the market and in local libraries. It is a convenient way to create prototypes or customized items, or to create replacement parts for household items (some of which are discussed in this book).

There are many types of 3D printing; however, the one discussed in this book is also referred to as additive manufacturing. The 3D printer essentially lays out material in two dimensions and then keeps adding layers on top of the previous layer to create a three-dimensional object. The material (filament) is fed into an extruder where it is heated to about 215°C, at which point it melts and the extruder pushes it out of a nozzle, much like toothpaste squeezed out of a tube. The extruder moves in three directions (left-right, front-back, and up-down) based on a sequence of commands that are determined based on the design. The design is usually created in a software separate from the printer (such as Tinkercad or Sketchup). The software file once completed is sent to the 3D printer software which interprets the software file that the 3D printer can understand. The printer software converts that into motion commands for the extruder. Most 3D printers will let you pause the printing midprinting this is a good way to see how the printer has determined the internal design of the object. Printers are shipped with various default settings to minimize the time and material to print objects. However, most printers will let users modify the default settings, so you can choose the temperature to heat the filament, the thickness of the outside walls, the amount of infill, the pattern of the infill, and other details.

3D PRINTING PROCESS

Typically, we use polylactic acid (PLA) plastic filament for printing, but this might vary slightly depending on the printer you use. There are many models of 3D printers, but in general, these are the steps necessary before printing a CAD creation:

- Ensure the bottom surface is touching the printing bed; if not, click the black arrowhead and drag it down till it indicates 0 mm (fig. 1).

- Export the design to the 3D printer.

- After the printer software has processed/sliced your design file, check to see whether the first layer of each element is sitting on the bed, or on another element (fig. 2).

- There should be NO overhangs greater than 30 degrees.

- Use a plastic file to remove any excess material.

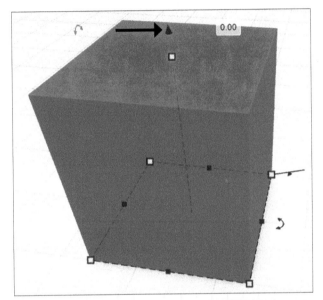

FIG. 1: *To ensure that the bottom of the print item is touching the printing bed, click and drag the black arrowhead to 0.*

FIG. 2: *Slice 1 on the printer bed.*

1

MAKING 3D PROJECTS WITH TINKERCAD

In this unit, we learn the basics of Tinkercad, a free, easy-to-use, online computer-aided design (CAD) program for designing objects for 3D printing. The program will help us develop our skills to design and create by modifying 3D basic shapes. We will create more than 20 projects, building on what we learn in each Lab to create objects that are increasingly complex. Let's get making!

GETTING STARTED WITH TINKERCAD

Tinkercad is computer-aided design (CAD) software used to create digital models in 3D by using its library of precreated 3D shapes. A Tinkercad account can be created online at Tinkercad.com, at no cost. Once you have created an account and logged in, you will be prompted by the software to go through a few tutorials. It is advisable to complete all these tutorials to familiarize yourself with the software.

After completing the tutorials, you will land on a page that gives you the option to **Create a New Design** (fig. 1). Click on this option.

This will bring you to the page where you will create your designs. Note the following parts of the page:

- In the top left corner is the file name. Tinkercad automatically creates a random name. Rename the file by clicking on it and typing in the name you want.

- The top ribbon directly under the file name has tools to **Copy**, **Paste**, **Duplicate**, **Delete**, **Undo**, and **Redo** work on the workplane. The arrow in fig. 2 identifies the top ribbon. Hover over a button to see its purpose.

- The right side of the top ribbon has more tools: **Group**, **Ungroup**, **Import**, **Export**, and others. See the right side of fig. 2.

FIG. 1: *Click on the **Create New Design** button to begin working in Tinkercad.*

FIG. 2: *The top ribbon has the file name and below that the **Copy**, **Paste**, **Duplicate**, **Delete**, **Undo**, and **Redo** buttons.*

- The left side of the page has the workplane viewing tools: **Zoom**, **Top View**, **Front View**, and **Home View**. See fig. 3 for details. Click on the views to explore.

- The central part of the page holds the **Workplane**. This is the main staging area where designs are created and manipulated using tools from various other parts of the page. The workplane is marked with a grid to assist in accurately placing designs and shapes on it. The scale of the grid can be modified using the **Edit Grid** button on the bottom right of the workplane. The arrow in fig. 4 marks the **Snap Grid** menu, which allows for variation in the magnitude of incremental dimension changes.

FIG. 3: *Along the left side are the* **Zoom**, **Top View**, **Front View**, *and* **Home View** *tools which control the view size and angle.*

FIG. 4: *The grid buttons control the workplane scale and dimension increments.*

The right side of the workplane has a variety of precreated tools that can be used to create various shapes. The drop-down menu can be used to access even more shapes than the basic shapes. There are also other tools, such as the **Ruler** on the right side (fig. 5).

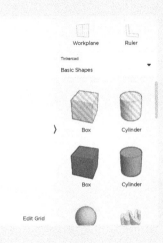

FIG. 5: *Precreated shapes and tools. The* **Ruler** *is also along the right side.*

There are various triggers that can be used to manipulate the size and orientation of shapes. Fig. 6 identifies some of the basic triggers. Arrow 1 identifies the black squares at the midpoint of each edge; this can be used to increase or decrease the length of a side/dimension, either by simply dragging it or by clicking on it and then entering the desired value for the side/dimension. Arrow 2 identifies the white squares at the corner of each shape. This can be used to modify the size of two dimensions simultaneously. Arrow 3 identifies the trigger that can be used to increase or decrease the height of the shape. Arrows 4, 5, and 6 are used to rotate the shape around different axes, while arrow 7 is used to move the shape vertically closer to or farther away from the workplane.

There are other tools and tips in Tinkercad that will grow your skills in computer-aided design, some of which will be discussed over the rest of this book. Continue to explore for yourself for different or easier ways to navigate the software.

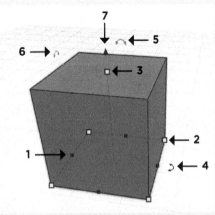

FIG. 6: *Triggers help you change size, orientation, and location of the shapes on the workplane.*

Basic Shapes with Straight Edges: Square Prisms

In our first Lab, we learn how to create basic two-dimensional (2D) and three-dimensional (3D) shapes using Tinkercad, then convert those designs into real objects that we can touch and hold by using a 3D printer.

A basic 3D shape with straight edges (such as a cube) has a size that is measured in length, width, and height. For shapes with curved edges (such as cylinders), the size of the curved part is determined by the "radius". We must remember these names as we will use them to discuss our objects and designs. Fig. 1 shows the measurement terms for the straight-edge shapes.

DESIGN NOTES

We will create two shapes/objects: one straight edged square prism and one straight edged square with specific measurements.

Square Prism—a cube that has been stretched in one direction.
Square—a cube that has been flattened.

THE DESIGN PROCESS

1. Start by drawing a sketch of a square prism (see fig. 1 for guidance).

2. Using the CAD software Tinkercad, create a cube with 20 mm sides by dragging and dropping a red box on the workplane from the **Basic Shapes** menu (fig. 2).

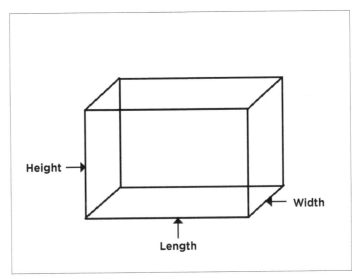

FIG. 1: *The dimensions of straight-edged shapes are length, width, and height.*

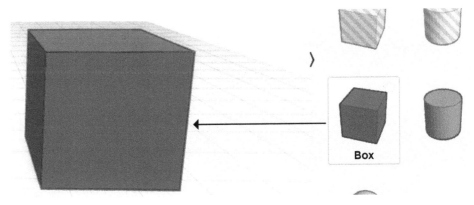

FIG. 2: *Selecting a red cube from the menu.*

3. Next, modify the size of the cube to make it a stretched cube, or square prism, 50 mm tall. Click and drag up the white square at the top of the cube to adjust height. The box will change color to red when selected (fig. 3).

4. Check the dimension of the sides to make sure they are still 20 mm by clicking on the small white square on any corner of the base (fig. 4).

5. Make a copy of the square prism from above or use a cube from the **Basic Shapes** menu.

6. Next, modify the size of the cube to make it 2 mm tall/thick (a flattened cube). Click and drag down the white square to adjust height (fig. 5).

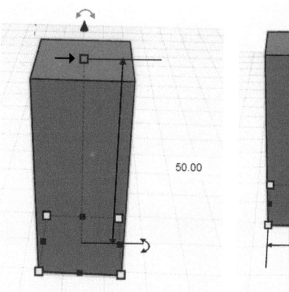

FIG. 3: *Click and drag the height button to stretch the cube upward.*

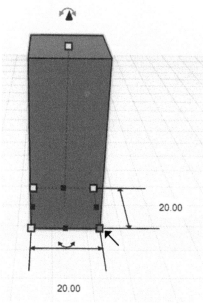

FIG. 4: *Clicking on the white square size adjusting tool on the corner shows the dimensions of the sides.*

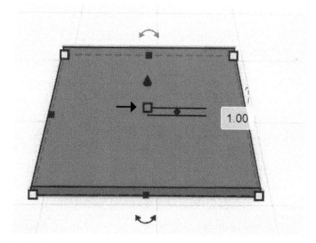

FIG. 5: *Drag the white square down to make the cube 2 mm tall.*

3D PRINTING CHECKLISTS

Before Printing Your CAD

- See 3D Printing Basics on page 9 for printing tips.

- Print the square prism.

- After printing, remove any excess material with a file.

Quality Control & Product Testing

- Inspect the printed object for the individual layers of plastic filament.

THINK ABOUT IT

Consider these questions and make notes about possible answers. You can test them by modifying and printing a new version of your design.

Is the printed object lighter or heavier than you expected? Why do you think it is so?

Did you get a chance to see the inside of the object as it was printing? What did it look like?

DESIGN CHALLENGE

Try to rotate the object in the CAD software so it is lying down along its longest side. You can do this by clicking on the curved arrowhead you think will make it rotate in the correct direction (see fig. 6—click and drag a circular arrowhead to turn object on its side). Do not worry if you turn it too much or in the wrong direction; simply click the **Undo** button till you get back to where you started. You can print this object too, but make sure to check that it is on the workplane before you try to print it.

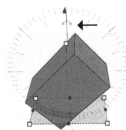

FIG. 6

THE SCIENCE BEHIND IT

There are multiple ways to create physical objects. In real life we start from a raw material, such as iron ore, that is converted into a semi-finished material, such as iron bars or sheet metal. We then shape the material using cutting, stamping, or welding to make our object of choice. The semi-finished materials usually come in the form of basic shapes, such as sheets, cubes, or cylinders. Later in this book we use basic shapes in our CAD software (Tinkercad) to design and print more complicated objects. But in this Lab, we only model and modify basic shapes themselves. As you modify the basic shapes, it might be helpful to think of them as a lumps of modeling clay that you are forming, stretching,or flattening.

LAB 2

Basic Shapes with Curved Edges: Cylinders

In this Lab we extend our basic skills to creating shapes with curved edges.

Remember that a basic 3D shape with straight edges, such as a cube, has dimensions measured in length, width, and height. For shapes with curved edges, such as cylinders, the size of the curved part is measured by the radius or diameter. The radius is the distance from the center of the base to the edge of the curve, and the diameter is two times the radius, or the distance from side to side running through the center. Learning these names will help you when designing curved objects. Fig. 1 shows the measurement terms for the curved-edge shapes.

DESIGN NOTES

We will create two shapes/objects: one cylinder and one circle with specific measurements.

Cylinder—a circle stretched to give it thickness
Circle—a flattened cylinder

THE DESIGN PROCESS

1. Start by drawing a sketch of a cylinder (see the fig. 1 for guidance).

2. Create a cylinder using the CAD software Tinkercad by dragging and dropping a cylinder on the workplane from the **Basic Shapes** menu (fig 2).

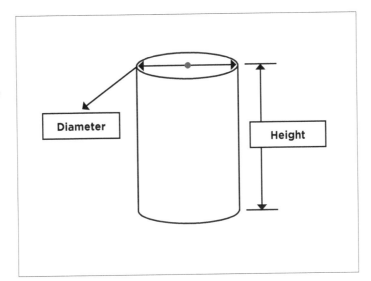

FIG. 1: *A cylinder sketch showing height and diameter.*

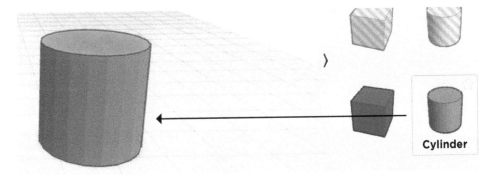

FIG. 2: *Selecting a* **Cylinder** *from the menu.*

3. Next, modify the size of the cylinder to make it 50 mm tall/high (a stretched cylinder). Click and drag up the white square at the top of the cylinder to adjust height. It will change color to red once you select it (fig. 3).

4. Check the dimension of the cylinder to makes sure it is 10 mm in radius (or 20 mm diameter) by clicking on the small black arrow on any bottom corner (fig. 4).

5. Make a copy of the cylinder from above or use a cylinder from the **Basic Shapes** menu.

6. Modify the size of the cylinder to make it 1 mm tall/thick (a flattened cylinder). Click and drag up the white square to adjust height (fig. 5).

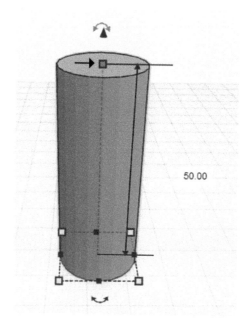

FIG. 3: *Click and drag the height button to change the height of the cylinder.*

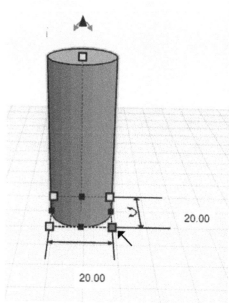

FIG. 4: *Click on the black square size adjusting tool on the bottom corner to see the diameter of the cylinder.*

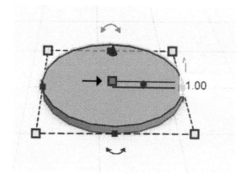

FIG. 5: *Use the height adjustment button to flatten the cylinder.*

3D PRINTING CHECKLISTS

Before Printing Your CAD

- See 3D Printing Basics on page 9 for printing tips.

- Print the cylinder.

- After printing, remove any excess material with a file.

Quality Control & Product Testing

- Inspect the printed object for the individual layers of plastic filament.

THINK ABOUT IT

Consider these questions and make notes about possible answers. You can test them by modifying and printing a new version of your design.

What do you notice about the curved face of the cylinder (its texture, its "roundness")?

Did you get a chance to see the inside of the object as it was printing? What did it look like?

DESIGN CHALLENGE

Try to rotate the object in the CAD software so it is lying down along its longest side. You can do this by clicking on the curved arrowhead you think will make it rotate in the correct direction (see fig. 6 from Lab 1—click and drag a circular arrowhead to turn object on its side). Do not worry if you turn it too much or in the wrong direction; simply click the **Undo** button till you get back to where you started. You can print this object too, but make sure to check that it is on the workplane before you try to print it.

THE SCIENCE BEHIND IT

A circle is made up of an infinite number of points. To print circular shapes, the printer software approximates a certain number of points on the circle and connects the points with plastic filament. The more points the software approximates on the circle, the closer to a perfectly round shape the print will be. In reality, a circle in printing is really a multisided polygon.

Tangram Puzzle

In this Lab we use the skills we learned to create basic shapes in Labs 1 and 2 to create complex shapes and make a tangram puzzle.

In Tinkercad, we can create complex shapes by simply creating two or more basic shapes, and then dragging them to touch or join each other. We will create a tangram geometric 2D puzzle to better understand this process.

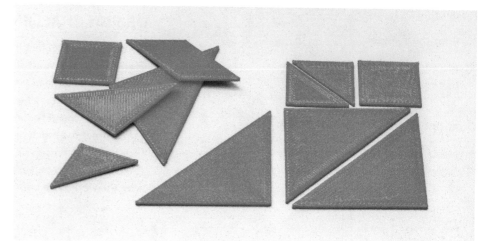

DESIGN NOTES

Tangrams are made up of seven pieces in specific proportion to one another. The small triangle is designed first and used as a measure for the other shapes (fig 1).

2 small isosceles triangles
1 medium isosceles triangle
2 large isosceles triangles
1 square
1 parallelogram

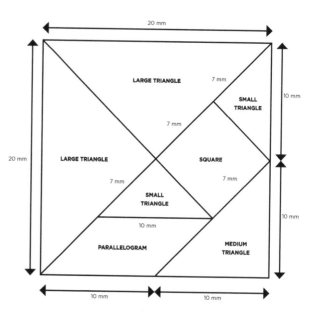

FIG. 1: *Dimensions for the Tangram Puzzle.*

THE DESIGN PROCESS

1. Create a small triangle by dragging a **Roof** onto the workplane from the shapes toolbox (fig. 2). The roof is a triangular prism.

2. Rotate the triangular prism onto its side so it lies flat as shown in fig. 3. Then flatten the triangular prism to a height of 3 mm.

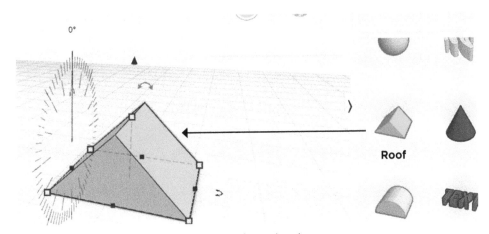

FIG. 2: *Drag a **Roof** onto the workplane from the shapes toolbox.*

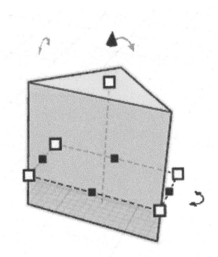

FIG. 3: *Rotate the triangular prism/roof so it is on its side.*

3. Now make sure the sides that form the right angles of the triangular prism are parallel to the gridlines on the workplane (fig. 4).

4. Enlarge the triangular prism so that both of the sides that form the right angle are 7 mm (fig. 5). Make a copy of this small triangle, and then move the two copies to one end of the workplane.

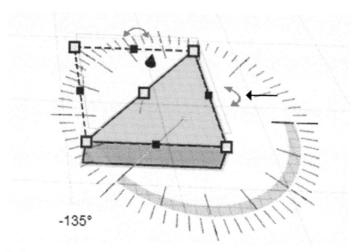

-135°

FIG. 4: *Align the right angle adjacent sides with the workplane gridlines.*

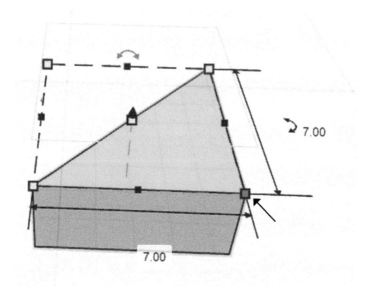

7.00

7.00

FIG. 5: *Adjust the size of the triangular prism sides to 7 mm.*

5. Repeat steps 1–4 from the small triangle to make the medium triangle.

6. Enlarge the small triangular prism so the two sides that form the right angle are 10 mm (fig. 6). Move it to one end of the workplane.

7. Make a copy of the medium triangular prism and enlarge it so the two sides that form the right angle are 14 mm. Make a copy of this large triangle, and then move the two copies to one end of the workplane.

8. Make the square by dragging a **Cube** onto the workplane from the shapes toolbox. Flatten the cube to a height of 3 mm.

9. Now make sure the sides that form the right angles of the cube are parallel to the gridlines on the workplane as we did in fig. 4.

10. Enlarge the cube so that each of the sides is 7 mm (fig. 6). Move it to one end of the workplane.

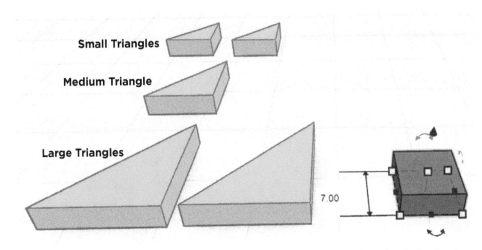

FIG. 6: *The various triangles and construction of the square using the* **Cube** *tool.*

11. Make the parallelogram by making two copies of the small triangles you made in the steps above. Rotate and merge them as shown in fig. 7.

12. Adjust the thickness of all triangles, square and parallelogram to be 3 mm.

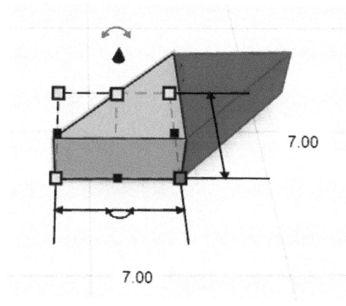

7.00

7.00

FIG. 7: *Rotate and merge two small triangles to form a parallelogram.*

3D PRINTING CHECKLISTS

Before Printing Your CAD

- See 3D Printing Basics on page 9 for printing tips.

- Print the tangram pieces.

- After printing, remove any excess material with a file.

Quality Control & Product Testing

- Inspect the printed object for the individual layers of plastic filament.

THINK ABOUT IT

Consider these questions and make notes about possible answers. You can test them by modifying and printing a new version of your design.

What was the strategy you used to put the puzzle together?

Are there any relationships among the pieces? If so, explain.

DESIGN CHALLENGE

Assemble all the tangram puzzle pieces together to form a square. Is there more than one way to form a square?

THE SCIENCE BEHIND IT

Isosceles triangles are triangles that have two equal sides. The two equal sides are also the sides that form the right angle in the triangle. The Tangrams is an ancient Chinese puzzle. Each piece is called a *tans*.

LAB 4

Designing Jewelry

In this Lab we learn how to remove material from a solid shape by creating holes. In Tinkercad, we can create a hole by simply using a **Hole** tool and inserting it into the desired location on a solid object. We will develop our skills creating holes in CAD by designing earrings.

DESIGN NOTES

We will create two designs as a stepping-stone to applying skills in designing utilitarian objects.

Creating a basic hole
Creating an earring

THE DESIGN PROCESS

1. Drag a **Solid Cube** onto the workplane. The dimensions do not matter for this example, but keep it small so it fits easily on the workplane.

2. Drag a **Cylinder Hole** onto the workplane to a point where it does not touch the initial cube (fig. 1). Make sure the height of the cylinder is much taller than the cube. Make sure the remaining dimensions of the cylinder are about half the cube.

3. Rotate the cylinder 90 degrees so it lies horizontal. Click on the curved **Rotate** tool (fig. 2).

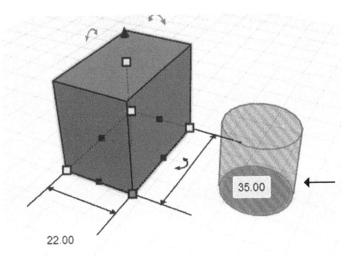

FIG. 1: *A cube and a cylinder hole on the workplane.*

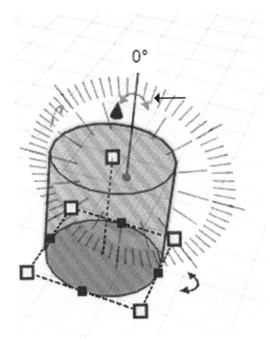

FIG. 2: *Click on the curved shape-rotate tool of the cylinder hole to rotate the cylinder.*

4. Now, move the cylindrical hole so it passes through the center of the side of the cube (fig. 3).

5. Select both objects and click the **Group** button (fig 4). This will merge the hole into the solid object, creating a hole in the solid object (fig. 5).

6. You can modify the circumference of the hole by modifying the length of the cylinder hole. Select the object and click on **Ungroup** to modify individual objects.

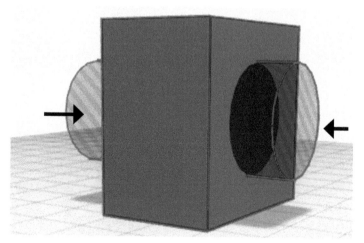

FIG. 3: *Position the cylindrical hole so it passes through the center of the cube.*

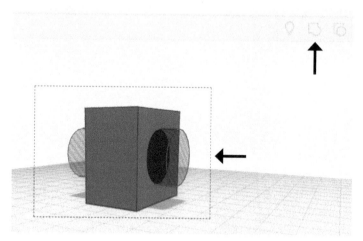

FIG. 4: *Group the cylinder hole and the cube.*

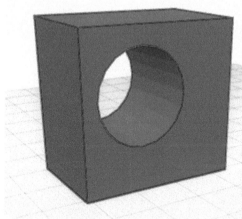

FIG. 5: *Now there is a round hole created in the solid cube.*

Creating an earring

1. The basic design of the earring we will make is shown in fig. 6. Note the basic elements: a solid shape of the earring, a big hole, and a small hole to attach the earring to the ear with a hook.

2. Drag a solid heart shape, from the **Basic Shapes** menu onto the workplane. The dimensions should be based on the size of the earring you want (fig. 7).

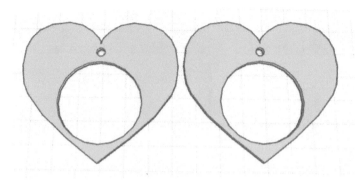

FIG. 6: *Three shapes make up the earring design: a heart, a large hole, and a small hole.*

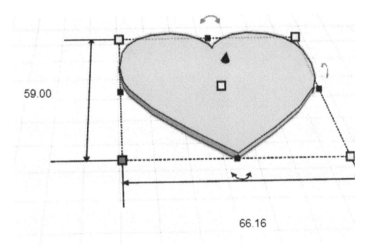

FIG. 7: *The solid heart-shaped earring on the workplane.*

3. Make a hole in this shape as big as possible following steps 2 through 5 on pages 31–32. No need to rotate it for the earring (fig. 8).

4. Make another small hole with a diameter of 2–4 mm in the center of the top of the heart. This is where we will put the hook to attach the earring to the ear (fig 9).

5. Select all the pieces and group them. Make a copy of the earring to create a pair of earrings.

FIG. 8: *Create a large hole in the solid heart.*

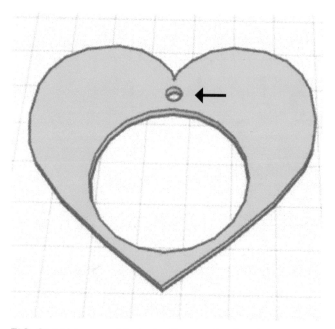

FIG. 9: *Make a small hole for the earring hook in the earring solid.*

3D PRINTING CHECKLISTS

Before Printing Your CAD

- See 3D Printing Basics on page 9 for printing tips.

- Print the earring set.

- After printing, remove any excess material with a file.

Quality Control & Product Testing

- Inspect the printed object for the individual layers of plastic filament.

THINK ABOUT IT

Consider these questions and make notes about possible answers. You can test them by modifying and printing a new version of your design.

Is there a limitation to the size of a hole in an object?

Can the hook hole be in a corner of the earring? Why? Or why not?

DESIGN CHALLENGE

Create a design to use as a ring that will fit your finger. Add some inscription to the ring by using premade letters in Tinkercad, like in Lab 10.

CONSIDERING CULTURE

Jewelry has been around for millenia. Initially metal jewelry was fitted on fingers and hooks by wrapping the metal around it tightly. It took many years for humans to master the technique of making a hole in metal.

Coat Hook/Curtain Tieback

So far we have covered designing complex shapes by adding two basic shapes together in Lab 3. We also learned how to remove material through the creation of holes in Lab 4. Now we will learn to design more complex shapes that involve adding and removing material in the same design. The object we will design is a coat hook, which can also be used as a curtain/drape holder. A curtain holder is the same shape as a coat hook but is oriented horizontally instead of vertically.

DESIGN NOTES

The strength of the hook depends on the design, material, and setting of the printer. Though it is usually strong, use caution in determining the load you hang on it.

A basic coat hook can be J-shaped and must have the following elements:

Stem, to rest against a wall or other surface (straight portion)
Curve, to hang the coat on
Holes, to attach the hook to a wall or other surface.

THE DESIGN PROCESS

1. Construct a stretched cube with a length of 70 mm and width and height of 10 mm each (fig 1). This is the stem of our J-shape.

2. Drag a **Donut Slice** onto the workplane (fig. 2). The donut slice tool can be found through the **Shape Generator** drop-down menu, under **All**. Scroll through until you get to the donut slice tool. Set the radius of the donut thickness as close to 5 mm as possible. Set the arc length to slightly more than 0.5. This will ensure your coat does not fall off the hook. Set the radius of the donut itself close to 20 mm. This donut slice will be the curve of the J-shape.

3. Move the donut slice curve to merge with the stem of the J-shape as shown in fig. 2. The coat hook designed thus far will have a tip of the same width as the body, which looks different from the image of the 3D-printed tappered-tip hook on page 36.

4. If the tapered hook is desired, we can do so by removing material from the tip using a **Rectangular Hole** tool.

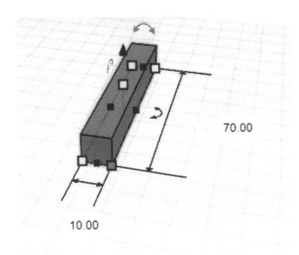

FIG. 1: *Create the stem of the coat hook by sizing a cube.*

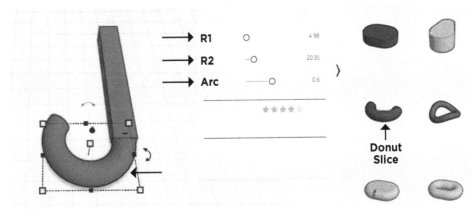

FIG. 2: *The donut slice makes the curved section of the hook.*

5. Now make two holes in the stem of the J-shape using the same process from Lab 4 (page 31–32). Each hole must be 5 mm in diameter and at least 2 mm from the edges. The holes must be at least 5 mm apart (fig. 3). The screws to attach the hook to the wall will go through these holes.

FIG. 3: *Create screw holes for the J-shaped hook.*

3D PRINTING CHECKLISTS

Before Printing Your CAD

- See 3D Printing Basics on page 9 for printing tips.

- Rotate the J-Shape so it is lying flat on the bed as in fig. 3.

- Print the coat hook.

- After printing, remove any excess material with a file.

Quality Control & Product Testing

- Take your product to a local hardware store to find screws that fit the holes.

- Inspect the product for: screw holes that accept the purchased screws, appropriate for the surface you plan on mounting the hook on.

- Test the product to make sure the hook holds a coat.

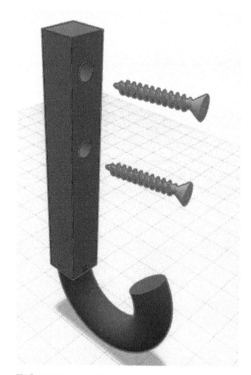

FIG. 4: *Insert the screws into the hook Screw holes to mount the hook.*

THINK ABOUT IT

Consider these questions and make notes about possible answers. You can test them by modifying and printing a new version of your design.

What would happen if the donut slice arc were 0.4 instead of 0.6?

Why should the holes be at least 2 mm from the edge?

DESIGN CHALLENGE

Sometimes the sharp edge of the donut slice might rip the coat fabric. How could you modify only one part of the design so the hook won't rip the fabric?

(Check out possible answers at the back of the book.)

THE SCIENCE BEHIND IT

Using two holes instead of one ensures that the coat hook does not rotate around one screw. It also increases the load-bearing capacity of the hook. Each screw has the ability to carry a certain load. Having two screws significantly increases the total capacity.

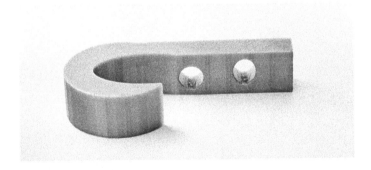

Local Architecture Project: Modeling Local Landmarks

Thus far we've learned to design complex shapes by adding and removing material. In this Lab you'll use your CAD modeling skills to replicate structures in your neighborhood.

We will follow a systematic approach that builds on the steps from the prior Labs. The idea is to develop an understanding of basic architecture, learn some local history, and improve our CAD skills.

The sample project features several buildings located in the Upper West Side of Manhattan, a neighborhood in New York City.

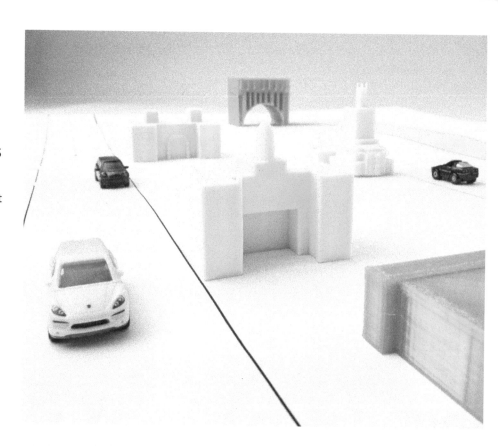

DESIGN NOTES

A basic local architecture project should include at least five structures set on a map of the neighborhood. Before starting the design process, we must identify the structures we want to model so we can decide on the size of the neighborhood map on which the models will sit.

MAP SIZE AND STRUCTURE SELECTION

1. Create a list of seven or eight structures in your neighborhood of architectural significance. Pick a couple of government buildings, schools/colleges, bridges, religious buildings, famous towers, stadiums, etc. First try to pick structures that are in close proximity to each other, then expand the search area if you need more structures.

2. Locate all the structures on a digital map, such as Google Maps.

3. Print the map to at least 2 feet by 3 feet/61 cm by 91.4 cm (you can print sections on regular letter paper and stick them together). You can print the map smaller or larger depending on your 2D printer. The idea is to make your structure roughly fit on its 2D-printed footprint. For example, a model of a school building cannot take up half the printed map.

4. Once you have printed the map, identify the length of the street/block(s) where your structure(s) will sit. This will help you determine the dimensions of your model. Write the block length.
Street/Block Length = _____ inches/cm
(typically not more than 2 inches/5.1 cm)

All structures will be broken down into the following sections: Foundation/Base, Body, Top/Roof/Tower, Façade, and Finer Elements (Windows, Doors, etc.).

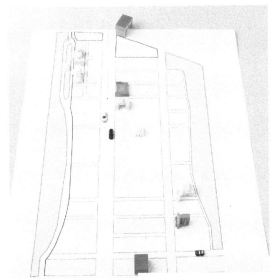

The completed 3D-printed models for the architecture project of New York City's Upper West Side in Manhattan placed on the map.

THE DESIGN PROCESS

1. For your first structure, identify the various parts (1-Base/Foundation, 2-Body, 3-Roof/Tower, 4-Facade/Finer Elements [windows, columns]) as shown in figs. 1 and 2, in which we identify the elements of Grant's Tomb and a bank in New York City as the design examples.

2. Decide the measurement of the longest side of the foundation/base (typically not more than 2 inches/5.1 cm). We chose 1 inch/2.5 cm for the tomb as our street length was 2 inches/5.1 cm, for a neighborhood size of about 50 inches/127 cm.

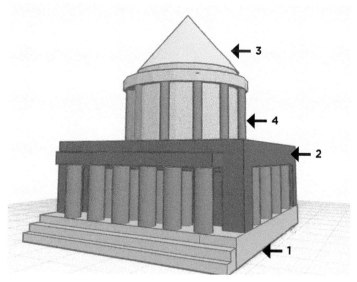

FIG. 1: *A CAD model of Grant's Tomb identifying the sections.*

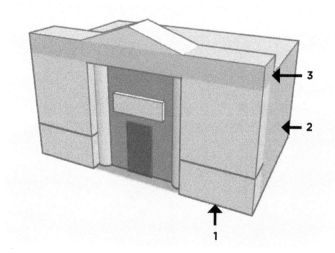

FIG. 2: *A CAD model of Apple Savings Bank identifying the sections.*

3. Decide on the width of the base and total structure height (must reflect the proportions of the real structure). We chose a little less than 1 inch, as the tomb is roughly square shaped.

4. Model each element of the structure in Tinkercad.

5. Model the remaining structures following steps 1–4.

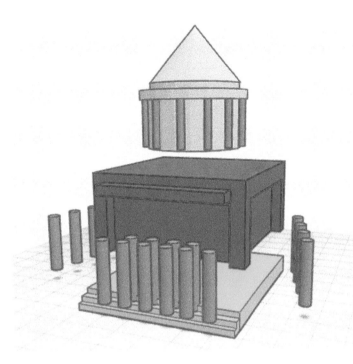

FIG. 3: *The various sections of Grant's Tomb being assembled.*

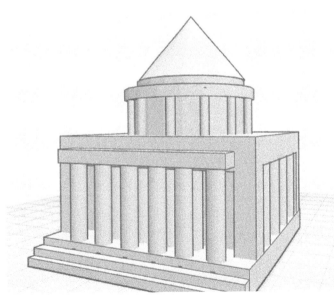

FIG. 4: *Image showing the assembled view of the various sections of Grant's Tomb.*

3D PRINTING CHECKLISTS

Before Printing Your CAD

▨ See 3D Printing Basics on page 9 for printing tips.

▨ After printing, remove any excess material with a file and place the structure on the map at appropriate location.

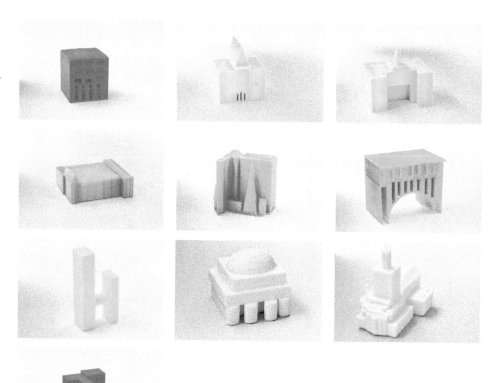

FIG. 5-14: *The completed 3D-printed models for the architecture project of New York City's Upper West Side.*

FIG. 15: *The completed 3D-printed models for the architecture project of New York City's Upper West Side neighborhood placed on the map.*

Quality Control & Product Testing

Inspect the print for:

- Proportions of the model match the real structure. Does any element of the model seem too big or small in comparison to the other element?

- Architectural similarity of each model to the real structure.

THINK ABOUT IT

Consider these questions and make notes about possible answers. You can test them by modifying and printing new versions of your designs.

Waht are two different architectural styles that are incorporated in your structures?

Why do you think one architectural style was selected over the other for these structures?

DESIGN CHALLENGE

Create a virtual walking tour of your local neighborhood using the map and models as props. Research the history of the structures. Invite friends/family to the tour that will inform them about the architecture and history of the structures they see every day.

CONSIDERING CULTURE

Structures hold a history of culture, trends, community, beliefs, environment, and technology prevalent at the time they were built. Learning about that can help us see the structures as objects of learning rather than simply places to stay. The same lessons can in turn inform the way we structure our lives today. For example, castles added gargoyles in medieval times as ornate drainpipes for rainwater, but also served as a way to ward off evil spirits. Similarly, we can design features into our structures that can serve dual purposes—practical and artistic.

LAB 7
Hair Comb

In this Lab, we switch gears from combining history, architecture, and CAD skills in learning about our neighborhood to exploring how to increase a material's flexibility by decreasing its rigidity. We'll design and print a hair comb to investigate this process.

DESIGN NOTES

Combs are among the oldest human inventions. Some early designs found in Africa dated to 1400 BCE look very similar to the combs we use today. Combs are easy to carry and very effective at untangling and parting hair. Generally, the denser or thicker the hair, the wider the spaces between teeth should be to prevent tangling. Some combs have a handle that ends in a point that can be used to create a parting, which increases the design's functionality.

A basic hair comb must have the following three elements:

Handle
Head
Teeth

For this Lab, we'll create a comb whose teeth are all the same size and evenly spaced.

THE DESIGN PROCESS

1. Use the **Box** and **Cylinder** tools to create a single tooth for the comb. Stretch the box to make it long and narrow. Stretch the cylinder to make it a little oblong. Then merge the two steps at the cylinder's widest point (also called its diameter). Dimensions should be about 2.5 mm thick and roughly an inch (2.5 cm) long. The cylinder gives the teeth a rounded edge to prevent them from hurting your scalp. Group the stretched box and stretched cylinder together to make a single tooth.

2. Make about 8 to 12 copies of the tooth and space them about 1.5 mm apart. Join the teeth at one end using the comb head. Create the head using a stretched box, which should be at least 2.5 mm thick and as long as needed to hold all the teeth (fig. 2).

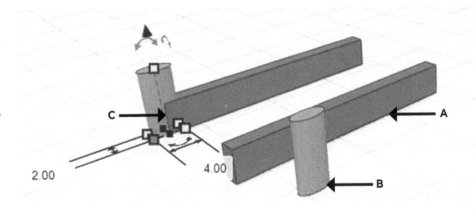

FIG. 1: *The stretched box (A), the stretched cylinder (B), and an assembled tooth at the widest point of the cylinder (C).*

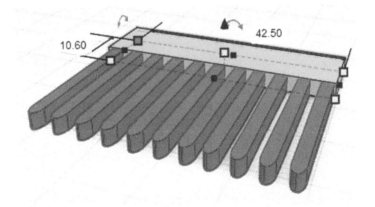

FIG. 2: *The stretched box for the comb head should be at least 2.5 mm thick and as long as needed to hold all the teeth.*

3. Create the handle using another stretched box that's the same thickness as the comb head and attach it to the head. The length of the handle is determined by the width of your palm, typically about 90 mm. Fig. 3 shows the handle and the cutout for the grip.

4. Fig. 4 shows the finished comb design. You can cut some shapes into the handle, either to decorate it or for a utilitarian purpose.

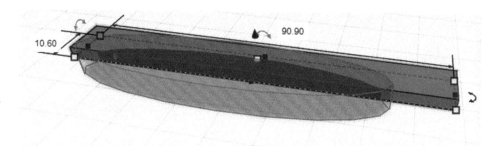

FIG. 3: *The comb's handle and the cutout for the grip.*

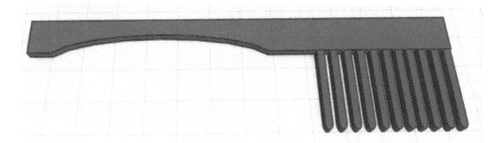

FIG. 4: *The completed comb design.*

DESIGN CHALLENGE

Can you design a handle for the comb for someone who lost their thumb? See page 141 for some potential solutions.

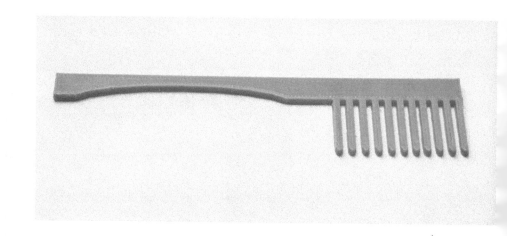

3D PRINTING CHECKLISTS

Before Printing Your CAD

- See 3D Printing Basics on page 9 for printing tips.

- Print the comb.

- After printing, remove any excess material with a file.

Quality Control & Product Testing

- Check to see if the teeth are flat or warped (turned upward). See fig. 5, which compares two combs: one with warped teeth, one with straight teeth. If the teeth are warped, change the design to thicken the teeth, and/or ensure all teeth are on the printing bed before reprinting.

- If the teeth are straight, remove any excess material with a file.

- Test the finished comb to see how easily it can be pulled through hair without getting stuck. Does it work with some types of hair, but not with others?

FIG. 5: *Check your print to see if its teeth are warped and adjust design as needed.*

THINK ABOUT IT

Consider these questions and make notes about possible answers. You can test them by modifying and printing a new version of your design.

What would happen if the teeth were 3 mm apart instead of 1.5 mm?

How many teeth would be too many for this comb?

Paperclip

In Lab 7 we created a comb that had teeth anchored on only one end, to give the other end of the teeth some flexibility to move during combing hair. In this Lab we extend the concept of creating flexibility in structures by removing anchoring parts. A paperclip is an ideal product that is rigid enough to hold a stack of papers together but also flexible enough to bend so it can clip onto the stack.

DESIGN NOTES

A basic paperclip has the following parts.

Top frame
Bottom frame
Frame connector

Sometimes the top and bottom frame can be considered to be a single piece with a gap notched out.

THE DESIGN PROCESS

1. In **Shape Generator—All** (arrow 1), use the **Smart Torus 2** (arrow 2) to create two tori, one smaller than the other and both of thickness 2 mm. The larger torus (arrow 3) should be roughly 75 mm by 35 mm, while the smaller (arrow 4) should fit inside it, roughly 50 mm by 20 mm (fig. 1).

2. Cut out a small portion at the top right-hand corner of the bigger torus using the **Hole** tool (fig. 2).

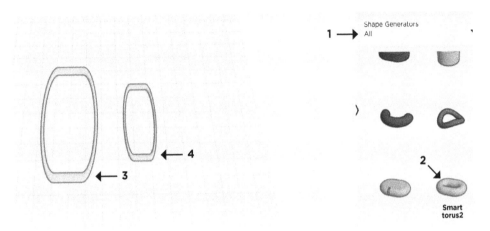

FIG. 1: *Model the paperclip using two torus shapes.*

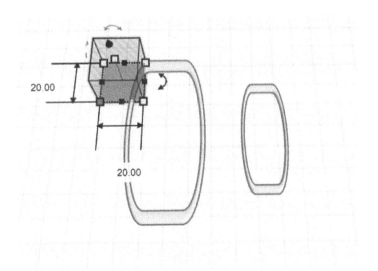

FIG. 2: *Cut out a portion of the larger torus using a box hole to increase the flexibility of the paperclip.*

3. Connect the two tori using a **Rectangular Bar** as shown in fig. 3.

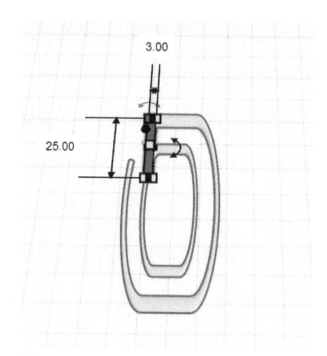

FIG. 3: *Connect the two tori with a* **Rectangular Bar** *to create the clip.*

3D PRINTING CHECKLISTS

Before Printing Your CAD

- See 3D Printing Basics on page 9 for printing tips.
- Print the paperclip.
- After printing, remove any excess material with a file.

Quality Control & Product Testing

- Test the product for its ability to hold a stack of papers together.

THINK ABOUT IT

Consider these questions and make notes about possible answers. You can test them by modifying and printing a new version of your design.

How could you modify the design to make the paperclip less flexible?

What modification would you make to the design to make the paperclip more flexible?

DESIGN CHALLENGE

Can you design a paperclip that has a wireframe of an animal, bird, or fish? (Check out possible answers at the back of the book.)

THE SCIENCE BEHIND IT

Paperclips are commonplace office items that temporarily hold a stack of papers together. Paperclips come in varying sizes, shapes, thickness, and designs. Gem-brand paperclips were the first modern wire paperclips, introduced in the late 19th century and made of a single metal wire. Modern 3D printing affords us the opportunity to customize this age-old device to suit our needs. The notch/gap creates flexibility in the clip. When paper is placed between the frames/tongues of the clip, they compress the paper and grip it tightly.

LAB 9

Pasta Spoon

Many of us enjoy a good bowl of pasta. However, making pasta is much easier if you have the right spoon, as pasta can be slippery and difficult to serve. In this Lab we design a pasta spoon with a hole. The hole can be used to measure a serving of pasta and for draining. But keep in mind that not everyone has the same serving size.

Note that the finished (smaller) printed spoon can only be used with cooled or cold pasta, but only to test it. Do <u>not</u> use it with hot pasta, or to serve pasta for eating.

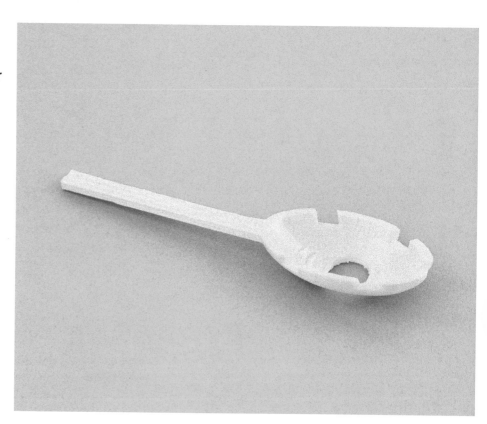

DESIGN NOTES

The typical pasta spoon has the following parts.

Spoon
Handle
Teeth
Hole (for measuring/draining)

THE DESIGN PROCESS

1. Using a **Half Sphere** tool, create two half spheres. The large solid-half sphere is about 30 mm × 30 mm, and the smaller one is a hole that is about 27 mm × 27 mm and shown in fig. 1.

2. Overlap the two spheres so they are concentric (with the smaller one inside the larger one). We are creating a spoon of wall thickness roughly 1.5 mm. Rotate the overlapping spheres together so the flat side is on top as shown in fig. 2.

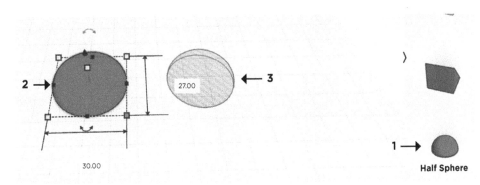

FIG. 1: *Create one solid half-sphere and one half-sphere hole for the dome-shaped section of the pasta spoon.*

FIG. 2: *Overlap the two spheres and rotate so the flat side is facing up.*

3. Group the two half-spheres and resize. The length should be about 55 mm, width 30 mm, and height about 13 mm as shown in fig. 3.

4. Now create three **Rectangular Hole-Bars** by stretching the **Box** tool. The width of each bar depends on how wide you want the gaps between the teeth of the pasta spoon to be. The image below shows them at 6 mm. Arrange them so the pasta spoon teeth will be approximately equally spaced (fig. 4).

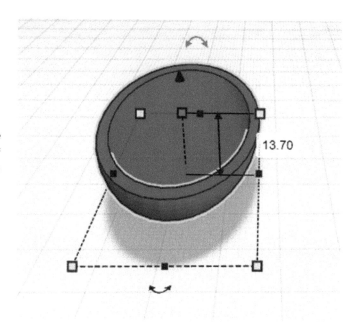

FIG. 3: *Group the half-spheres and resize.*

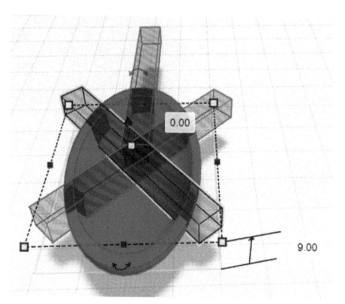

FIG. 4: *Use rectangular hole-bars to create the teeth of the pasta spoon.*

5. Group all the hole-bars and spoon together with the **Group** tool to get a spoon with teeth as shown in fig. 5.

6. Create a hole in the center of the spoon using a **Cylindrical Hole** tool (fig. 6).

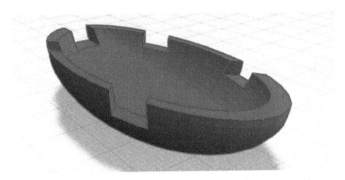

FIG. 5: *Group the hole-bars and spoon spheres together.*

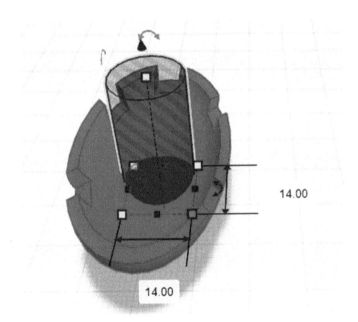

14.00

14.00

FIG. 6: *Use a cylindrical hole to make the hole in the middle of the spoon.*

7. Group the cylindrical hole and the spoon to complete the hole in the spoon. Add a handle as shown in fig. 7.

8. Rotate the entire design 180 degrees so it lies flat (face down) on the workplane. This will be the orientation for printing.

FIG. 7: *Add a handle and group all the pieces together.*

THINK ABOUT IT

Consider this questions and make notes about possible answers. You can test them by modifying and printing a new version of your design.

How could you modify the design to make the pasta spoon grab wet pasta better?

3D PRINTING CHECKLISTS

Before Printing Your CAD

- See 3D Printing Basics on page 9 for printing tips.

- Print the pasta spoon.

- After printing, remove any excess material with a file.

Quality Control & Product Testing

- Test the product for its ability to grab wet pasta. **DO NOT USE WITH HOT PASTA and DO NOT USE TO SERVE FOOD.**

DESIGN CHALLENGE

Modify the handle of the pasta spoon so it is easier to grip; this is called *ergonomic*.

CONSIDERING CULTURE

Pasta was eaten mostly by hand until the 19th century, when the introduction of tomato sauce made it even more challenging to grip. Forks were initially developed with four curved prongs. One of the earliest recorded patent for a "culinary server" with multiple curved prongs was recorded in 1856. Since then "macaroni servers" have been developed with prongs on one or both sides of the serving spoon. The prongs help to grip the pasta or spaghetti while it is being twirled during serving. Holes in the bowl of the spoon were also developed to permit drainage of the water. The hole can also be used to measure portions of pasta for cooking. Some experiments have suggested a pasta spoon length of about 10 inches/25.4 cm with a slightly angled bowl and a small hole is most efficient for serving pasta.

LAB 10
Crushing the Alphabet: Testing Structural Strength

Having honed our skills in manipulating material shapes and sizes in the previous Labs, we will now explore how the strength of simple structures is impacted by the structure's orientation. Different structures are stronger/less flexible depending on which way the parts under stress are oriented.

This Lab requires the use of a mechanical vise, which can be found at most major hardware stores for a reasonable price, and safety glasses during the testing process. Optional: You may also choose to use a force meter to obtain more accurate readings. Shown is the Nextech DFS500 Digital Force Gauge.

DESIGN NOTES

We will create a variety of letters from the alphabet, print them using a 3D printer, and then test them for structural strength across different orientations. The strength can be assessed using one of two ways depending on the detail desired—by visual deformation of a structure or by using a force meter. The objective is to identify the points of weakness in different letters and different orientations of those letters.

THE DESIGN PROCESS

1. Choose a variety of letters of different shapes, such as A, B, C, and T.

2. Design these shapes using the **Text and Numbers** tool on the same workplane. The length of each letter should be 20 mm, height 3 mm, and the width should be in proportion to the shape of the letter (fig. 1).

3. Adjust the print properties/configurations to ensure that shapes have 5 percent infill prior to starting printing (see your 3D printer settings for this). Print two of each shape.

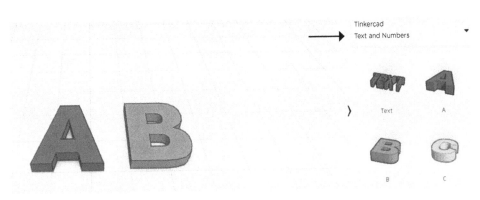

FIG. 1: *Tinkercad has tools for letters and numbers.*

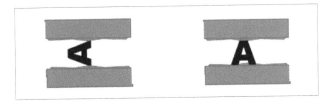

FIG. 2: *Position letters in the vise jaws, first along their length, then their width, to test the properties of each letter in different orientations.*

3D PRINTING CHECKLISTS

Before Printing Your CAD

- See 3D Printing Basics on page 9 for printing tips.

- Print two of each letter.

- After printing, remove any excess material with a file.

STRENGTH TESTING PROCESS

Wear SAFETY GLASSES during this process!

1. Mount the mechanical vise on a stable table.

2. Place the first letter laterally in the vise along its width till the vise jaws grip it, but not so tight as to deform the letter. See fig. 2, which shows the letter A placed in the vise jaws along its length in the first part, and along its width in the second part.

3. As you start to turn the vise handle:
   • Note the number of turns till the letter begins to deform
   • Note the section of the letter that deforms—top, bottom, middle, stem of the letter, curve of the letter
   • Note the direction of deformation—horizontal, vertical, or diagonal

4. Use a new print of the same letter, but this time, place it in the vise in a different orientation, along its length (fig. 2), till the vise jaws grip it, but not so tight as to deform the letter (fig. 3).

5. Record the deformation information from Step 3 in a table like the one shown below. Your data will vary depending on material and size of printed letter as well as the type of vise used.

FIG. 3: *The letter E placed in the vise jaws along its length.*

RESULTS FOR LETTER DEFORMATION

Letter	Orientation	# of handle turns to start Deformation	Section deformed	Direction of deformation
T	Along length	5	Central stem of T	Horizontal
T	Along width	6	Top stem of T	Horizontal
E	Along length			

THINK ABOUT IT

Consider these questions and make notes about possible answers. You can test them by modifying and printing new versions of your designs.

Do any letters return to their original shape after they are taken out of the vise? If so, why?

DESIGN CHALLENGE

Modify the letter O to make it more resistant to deformation.

THE SCIENCE BEHIND IT

The shapes of letters in the alphabet are used to design many structures around us. An I-beam is commonplace in many construction projects. H-shaped structures are commonly used in tunnel construction to support the tunnel and maximize road space. C-shaped structures are used to create arches in construction projects because of their uniform distribution of weight. The force exerted by real-world loads can be simulated using a vise. A force sensor/ tester can be used together with a vise to measure the actual force applied to deform the letters (fig. 4).

FIG. 4: *You can use a force sensor to measure the force applied by the vise against the letters.*

LAB 11

Artificial Coral Reef

In the first ten Labs we learned about various design techniques by adding, removing, merging, and resizing material. We'll now explore more complex techniques in which we adapt our designs to interact with other materials/environments.

This Lab involves adapting a design that is placed in water so that we can modify the flow of water around it. This will be accomplished through a project to design an Artificial Coral Reef. A coral reef shelters small fish and also causes disturbances in flowing water, that slow it down, so the coral and the fish can grab food/nutrients from the water. We can test the coral reef design using flow simulation software.

DESIGN NOTES

The basic artificial coral reef has the following features:

Frame
Small nooks/crevices (to provide shelter for small fish)
Protrusions/traps (to slow down/modify the flow of water)

THE DESIGN PROCESS

1. The frame of the coral reef can be of any shape, including nonbasic shapes. In our example, we will use a rectangle-based frame with horizontal and vertical holes as shown in fig. 1. Typically, no dimension should be greater than 50 mm. The holes can be of any shape. We have chosen rectangular holes as seen in figs. 1 and 2.

2. Create an offset hole in the central beam. Again, this hole can be located in any corner and can be of any shape. The objective is to make the water that enters the frame change direction and slow down (fig. 3).

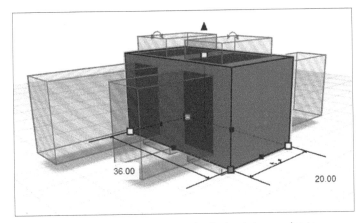

FIG. 1: *Slide numerous rectangular holes into a cube to design a coral reef model.*

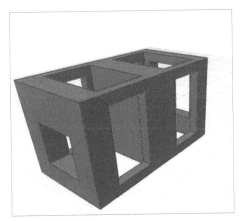

FIG. 2: *Group the holes and the cube.*

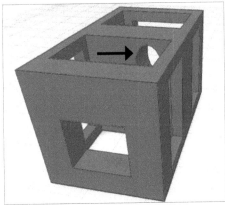

FIG. 3: *Add an offset hole in the central beam.*

3. Add assorted shapes to the frame to partially block some big holes (to keep the bigger fish out) and also to create nooks that will change the direction of the flow of water and slow it down. See fig. 4 where arrows 1 and 2 show small nooks in the reef.

4. Optional: Download a copy of the .STL file from Tinkercad and load it into the Autodesk Flow Design software, which simulates liquid flowing through the design. Adjust the source of the flow to line up (Fig. 5, arrow 1) with the reef model (Fig. 5, arrow 2). Start the flow and observe how it changes due to the design of the reef. Observe whether there are any blue streaks (Fig. 5, arrow 3). This indicates that the water particles have been slowed down significantly. See fig. 5 for a view of a simulation.

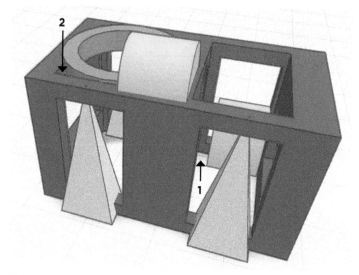

FIG. 4: *Use a variety of shapes to create nooks in the coral reef.*

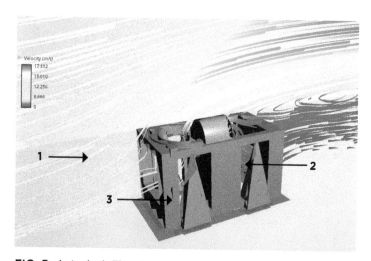

FIG. 5: *Autodesk Flow Design software simulates the flow of liquid through the coral reef. Dark blue indicates the flow that has slowed down the most.*

3D PRINTING CHECKLISTS

Before Printing Your CAD

- See 3D Printing Basics on page 9 for printing tips.

- Print the Artificial Coral Reef.

- After printing, remove any excess material with a file.

Optional Quality Control & Product Testing

- Test the CAD model using the Autodesk Flow Design software.

THINK ABOUT IT

Consider this question and make notes about this possible answers. You can test them by modifying and retesting a new version of your design.

How does the coral reef structure slow down the water in the reef?

DESIGN CHALLENGE

Modify your design so the slow-moving water will be just outside the main frame of the reef.

THE SCIENCE BEHIND IT

Due to the loss of coral reefs in the oceans, a lot of artificial coral reefs are being deployed. These reefs are made out of various artificial materials, such as concrete pod arrays, old subway cars, and networks of car tires. In addition, 3D-printed artificial coral reefs are used in several places around the world.

The introduction of an object in the path of flowing water causes the water molecules to change direction. This slows them down and correspondingly slows other molecules down too (breaks the flow).

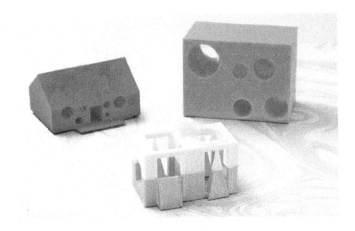

LAB 12

Whistle Design

In the previous Lab we designed an artificial coral reef structure to modify the flow of water. In this Lab we design a structure that will modify/direct the flow of air. A whistle channels the air blown through it so as to flow over an edge to create a sound. Designing a whistle in CAD is a complex process requiring multiple steps.

DESIGN NOTES

A basic whistle has the following parts:

Body
Mouthpiece hole
Sound hole
Whistle pea

THE DESIGN PROCESS

1. Use a **Cylinder** tool to create the whistle body 27 mm in diameter and 20 mm tall. Add a **Box** at the top left corner that is the same height as the cylinder, 20 . mm, but 7 mm wide and about 25 mm long. Make sure the box is flush with the cylinder where they meet. Fig. 1. arrow 1 shows the point where they touch. **Group** the cylinder and box together.

2. Now we will hollow out the whistle body. Create another cylinder with diameter 23 mm. Move it so it fits inside the cylinder from step 1 evenly on all sides (concentric). Add another box that is 4 mm wide and a little longer than the box in step 1. Line up the box and cylinder in step 2 so they flush just as we did in step 1 (fig. 2). Group the box and cylinder in step 2 and convert to a hole. Move it off the workplane by 2 mm. Then, group the box and cylinder In steps 1 and 2 to form the hollowed-out whistle body. See fig. 3 and note the flush joint of the box and cylinder marked by arrow 1.

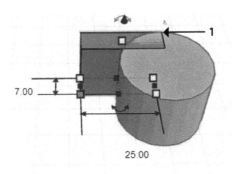

FIG. 1: *Connect the cylinder and box of the whistle body.*

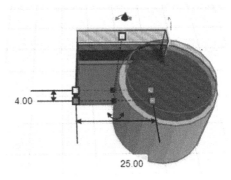

FIG. 2: *Use a cylinder hole and box hole to hollow out the whistle body.*

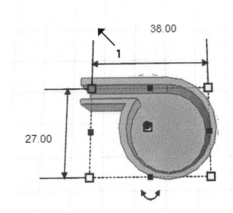

FIG. 3: *Note the flush joint of the box and cylinder.*

3. The mouthpiece hole needs to be tapered on the inside. Use the **Wedge** tool
from the **Basic Shapes** toolbox to create
a wedge that will attach to the inside of
the mouthpiece to taper it. The wedge
should be rotated as shown in fig. 4. It
should be about 1.50 mm thick at the
broader end (arrow 1 in fig. 4). Attach
it to the inside of the mouthpiece hole
as shown. Adjust the **SnapGrid** so you
can make modifications by less than
1 mm. There should be no gaps between
the wedge and the lower face of the
mouthpiece it attaches to. See fig. 4
for details.

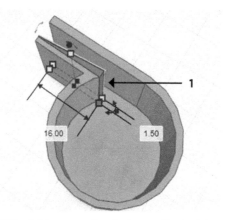

FIG. 4: *Use a wedge to taper the inside of the whistle mouthpiece.*

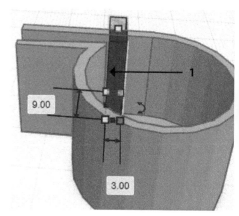

FIG. 5: *Create and align a sound hole for the whistle.*

4. Create the whistle sound hole. First,
we will create a hole at the top of the
whistle. Use the **Box** tool to make a box
hole that is 3 mm wide and 18 mm high
(fig. 5). Move it so it is about in line with
the broader end of the wedge from the
mouthpiece hole (arrow 1). Move it so
that it is 2 mm above the workplane.
Group it with the whistle body.

5. Now we need to taper the edge of the
sound hole that is further away from
the mouthpiece. Use the **Wedge** tool to
create a wedge hole as shown in fig. 6. It
will have to be rotated along a couple of
axes to orient it as shown in the image.
It should be 3.8 mm at the broader end.
Make sure to align it so the narrower
end meets the whistle body at a single
edge as shown in fig. 6. Merge the
wedge hole with the whistle body.

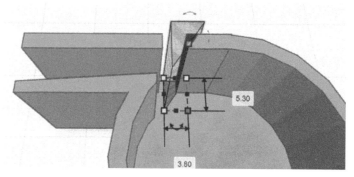

FIG. 6: *Taper the edge of the sound hole using a wedge hole.*

6. Design the whistle pea by creating a **Sphere** 15 mm in diameter and locate it 1.9 mm above the workplane. It should be inside the whistle as shown in fig. 7.

7. Use the copy we made earlier of the whistle body cylinder and box in step 1. Flatten it to 2.1 mm and align it to cover the whistle design from step 6. Move it so that it is 18.9 mm above the workplane, to ensure there are no gaps. Group it with the whistle body to complete the design. See fig. 8 for the completed whistle.

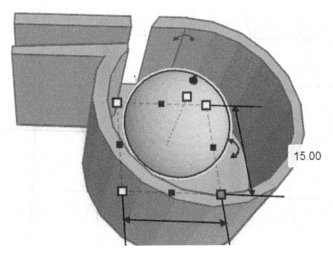

15.00

FIG. 7: *The whistle pea is a sphere inside the whistle.*

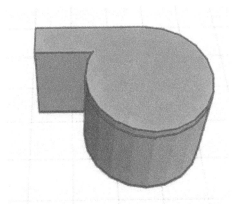

FIG. 8: *Complete the whistle by making a cover using the flattened copy of the whistle body.*

Basic Dovetail Joint

Sometimes we require our designs to be flexible structures so we can increase/decrease motion and/or assemble/disassemble them to meet the functionality and/or printing limitations. Joints, similar to the ones in our bodies, can be used for this purpose. There are many different types of joints. Some restrict motion in a particular direction like the knuckles in our fingers; others permit rotational motion like the ones in our shoulders. In this Lab, we will use a dovetail joint to limit motion in one direction so we can assemble and disassemble two parts.

DESIGN NOTES

The basic dovetail joint has two parts that slide into each other along only one axis:

Dovetail-shaped notch or socket

Dovetail-shaped protrusion or tail

THE DESIGN PROCESS

1. Model the socket section of the dovetail joint. Use the **Box** tool to create a 20 mm by 35 mm box, 12 mm high.

2. Use the triangular prism **Roof** tool to create the dovetail-shaped socket in the box. The roof should be smaller in width than the box by at least 2 mm. For this project, that is 12 mm. The height should be about the same as the box. Move the roof to center it about the width of the box, and less than halfway in from the top of the box (fig. 1). Arrow 1 shows that the roof is less than halfway in the box, which is important.

3. Convert the roof to a hole and group with the box to complete the socket section of the joint (fig. 2). It should look like a through hole in the box that's shaped like a dove's tail.

4. Start the tail section of the joint by using the **Box** or **Cylinder** tool to create a solid shape 20 mm long and 15 mm high.

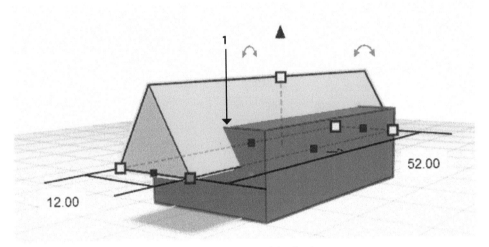

FIG. 1: *Position the triangular prism (roof) inside the box.*

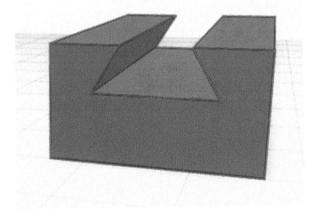

FIG. 2: *Grouping the triangular prism and the box creates a dovetail-shaped socket/notch.*

5. Use the **Roof** tool to create a second roof that is 2 mm narrower than the roof we used for the socket section in step 2 above. The height should be 1 mm shorter (fig. 3).

6. Merge the second roof with the box/cylinder from step 4. It should have less than half the roof embedded in the box/cylinder so it can slide into the socket section. The arrow 1 in fig. 3 shows that less than half of the roof is embedded in the box of the tail section.

7. Group the roof and the box/cylinder from step 4 to complete the tail section. Move it in position to mate with the socket section so you can check the fit. Fig. 4 shows an incorrect fit on the left (arrow 1) and the correct fit on the right (arrow 2 shows the slight gap between the tail and socket sections of the joint). The gap shown by arrow 3 will not impact the joint as much and can be less than 1 mm.

8. After testing the fit and adjusting the dimensions if needed, move the tail section away from the socket section, so they are separated for printing. If you used a box in step 4, you will need to rotate the tail section 90 degrees so it is standing up on its end (fig. 5). This will ensure there are no overhangs during the printing process.

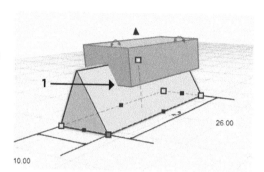

FIG. 3: *Create a slightly narrower tail that will slide into the socket.*

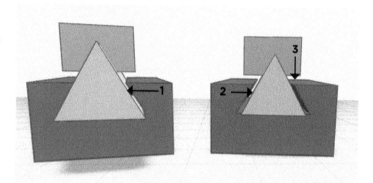

FIG. 4: *Slide the grouped tail section into the socket. The correct fit has a slight gap.*

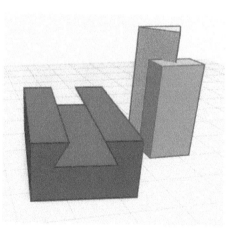

FIG. 5: *The completed design positioned for 3D printing.*

3D PRINTING CHECKLISTS

Before Printing Your CAD

- See 3D Printing Basics on page 9 for printing tips.

- Print the dovetail joint.

- After printing, remove any excess material with a file.

Quality Control & Product Testing

- Test the design to see whether the two sections can slide into and out of each other.

THINK ABOUT IT

Consider this questions and make notes about possible answers. You can test them by modifying and printing a new version of your design.

Why do we need the dimensions of the tail section to be slightly smaller than the socket section?

DESIGN CHALLENGE

Modify your design so the two sections can only slide in from one side.

THE SCIENCE BEHIND IT

While joints are generally associated with restricting motion, a nonrigid joints such as a dovetail joint can be used to increase functionality due to its ability to selectively permit motion along a single straight line. Some joints will only permit rotational movement and not any straight-line motion.

Phone Holder

In Lab 13 we were introduced to dovetail joints. As a reminder, joints are useful to connect two or more objects together to create a larger object. In this project, we solidify this skill by designing a product that requires a dovetail joint—collapsible cellphone stand. Allowing the cellphone stand to collapse makes it easier to carry.

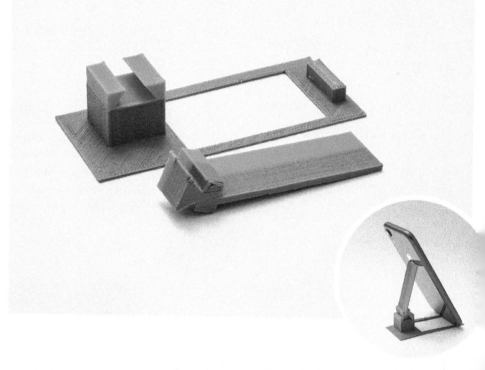

DESIGN NOTES

The basic cellphone stand must have the following elements:

Base, for the phone to sit on and to mount other parts of the stand
Backrest, for the phone to lean against at different angles

Lip, to keep the phone from sliding while resting backrest-to-base connection joint, so the stand is collapsible

Refer to Lab 13, Basic Dovetail Joint (page 72), for how to create the dovetail joint.

THE DESIGN PROCESS

1. We begin the design process with a rough sketch of what we'd like the cellphone stand to look like with the four elements mentioned in the design notes. Use fig. 1 as a guide, but you can vary some aspects, such as the shape of the lip, backrest, and base.

2. Next, we model the elements of the product from the sketch in step 1 using the CAD software.

Create the base (thickness 2 mm, width about 40 mm, length about 80 mm [#2 in fig. 2]).

Create the lip (about 2 mm height above base, length is about 10 mm [#1 in fig. 2]).

Create the socket section of the dovetail joint, attached to the base, about 20 mm on longest side, or one-half the width of the base (#3 in fig. 2).

Create the tail section of the dovetail joint sized to match socket (#4 in fig. 2).

Create the backrest/stand and attach it to the tail part of the dovetail joint (20 mm wide backrest [#5 in fig. 2]).

Add a cut-out in the base. This is not necessary, but can save material. See fig. 3 for details. The size of the cut-out can vary depending on the amount of material you want to save.

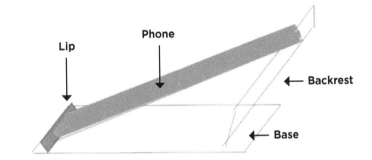

FIG. 1: *A rough sketch of a cellphone stand with a phone.*

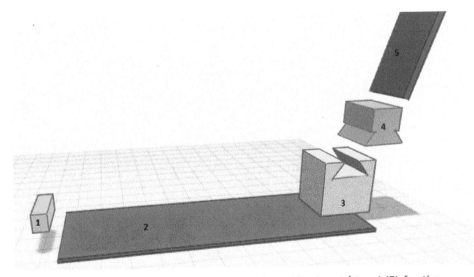

FIG. 2: *The lip (1), base (2), socket (3), tail (4), and backrest/stand (5) for the cellphone stand with a dovetail joint.*

3D PRINTING CHECKLISTS

Before Printing Your CAD

- See 3D Printing Basics on page 9 for printing tips.

- Rotate the backrest-dovetail joint tail section so it is lying flat on the bed (fig. 4).

- Consider creating some holes, to save material (see the rectangular-shaped hole in the base in fig. 3).

- Ensure that the dimensions of the tail section of the dovetail joint are slightly smaller than the dimensions of the socket section of the joint.

- Print the phone holder.

- After printing, remove any excess material with a file.

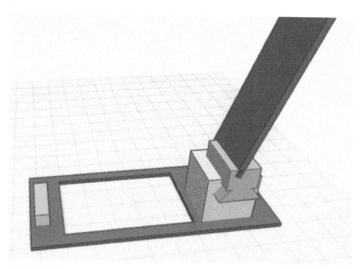

FIG. 3: *The assembled view of the cell phone holder.*

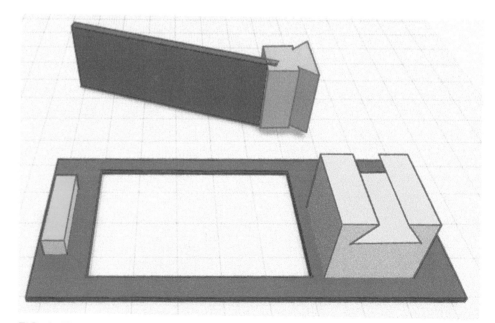

FIG. 4: *The completed cell phone holder design positioned for 3D printing.*

Quality Control & Product Testing

Test the product for:

- Ability of the joint to work smoothly for assembly and disassembly.

- Ability for a phone to be held upright by the stand.

THINK ABOUT IT

Consider these questions and make notes about possible answers. You can test them by modifying and printing a new version of your design.

How does the lip help the design objectives?

How did you/could you adapt your design to make it as flat as possible when disassembled?

DESIGN CHALLENGE

Can you modify only one part of the design so the phone holder can hold the phone upright at more than one position?

THE SCIENCE BEHIND IT

The dovetail joint helps to attach the backrest to the phone base. This permits the weight of the phone to prevent the backrest from pulling the rest of the stand to topple over. The height of the backrest is a fine balance between the location of the center of gravity of the phone and the desired angle of viewing the screen.

Camera Holder with Ball-and-Socket Joint

In Lab 14 we used a dovetail joint that could be disassembled to increase functionality. Now, we will use a different joint, the ball-and-socket joint, to allow rotation for a camera holder. We will use a slotted socket as this permits for greater tolerances in design.

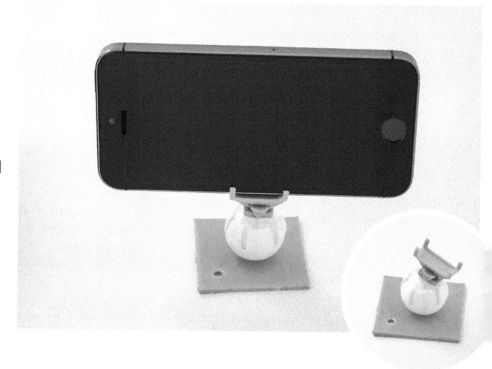

 DESIGN NOTES

A basic slotted ball-and-socket joint camera holder has the following parts:

Slotted socket with base
Ball
Camera mount

THE DESIGN PROCESS

Creating a slotted socket with base

1. Create a sphere, 25 mm diameter, using the **Sphere** tool. Then slice about ¼ off the top using a **Rectangular Hole** tool as shown in fig. 1. Group the rectangular hole and the sphere together to get the initial socket frame (fig. 2).

2. Now we will hollow out the socket frame. Create a **Sphere Hole** with 23 mm diameter. Move it so it fits inside the sphere from step 1 evenly on all sides (concentric) (fig. 2). Group the internal hole-sphere and external socket spheres to form the hollowed-out socket.

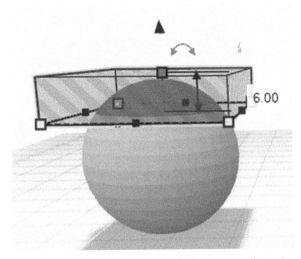

FIG. 1: *Position a rectangular hole over a sphere to slice off the top of the sphere.*

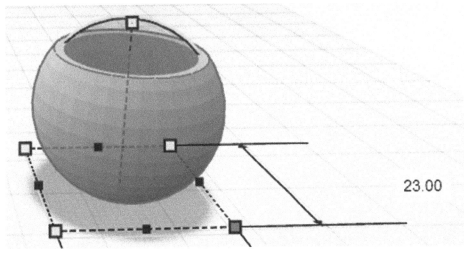

FIG. 2: *Group the rectangular hole and the sphere.*

3. Now we will create slots in the wall of the socket so that it is flexible to allow the ball to insert into it. Create a **Rectangular Prism Hole** and orient it as shown in fig. 3. Care should be taken so that the slot goes till about halfway down the height of the socket. Create two more slots as shown in fig. 3.

4. **Group** the slot holes and the hollow socket to complete the socket frame. Move the entire socket up vertically by 1 mm and add a 2 mm base right below it as shown in fig. 4.

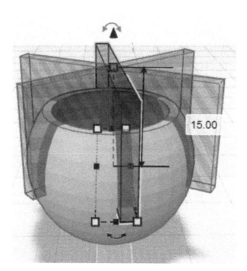

FIG. 3: *Use rectangular holes to cut the slots into the hollowed-out sphere.*

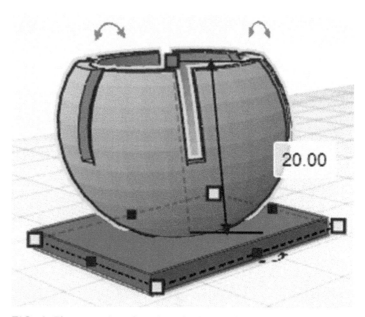

FIG. 4: *The completed socket design with grouped slot holes and spheres resting on a base.*

5. To create the ball for the joint, simply use the **Sphere** tool to create a ball that is 1 mm less than the internal diameter of the socket. We used 22 mm for the ball diameter. Add a small box to use as the handle for the ball at the top (fig. 5).

6. The camera mount will have to be created as a separate piece so it can be 3D printed easily. The camera mount is a basic cradle that holds the camera in it with a press fit. Simply create a camera mount that attaches to the ball handle using a dovetail joint from Lab 13 (page 72). This will require two parts: the dovetail joint mate and the cradle. The dovetail joint mate (arrow 2 in fig. 6) that attaches to the cradle is created using a **Double Trapezoid** tool from the **Shape Generators Tool Box** (arrow 1 in fig. 6).

7. The cradle is created using multiple **Box** tools to create the shape shown by arrow 3 in fig. 6. The camera will fit snugly in the cradle, so the width of the cradle should match the thickness of your camera (about 7 mm for some cellphone cameras). Then merge the cradle and the cradle mating double trapezoid from step 6 (fig. 6).

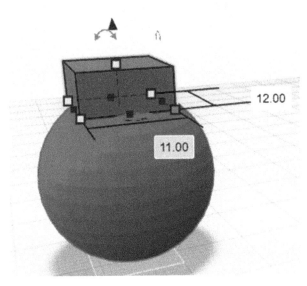

FIG.5: *Create the ball for the joint and add a box for the handle.*

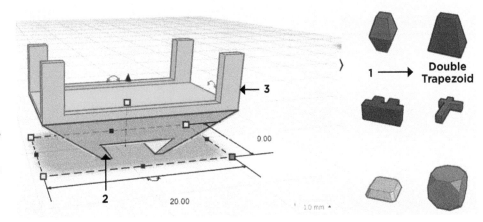

FIG. 6: *The camera holder cradle with a dovetail joint section created using a double trapezoid.*

8. The socket/notch in the dovetail joint
   mate and the tail on the handle (fig. 7)
   are created using the dovetail joint
   creation steps in Lab 13 (page 72).

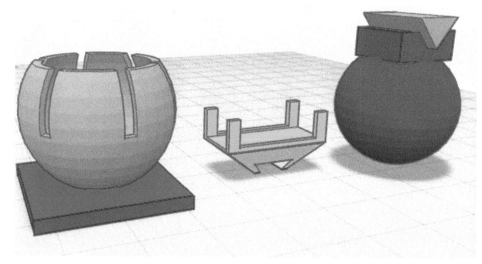

FIG. 7: *Positioning the camera holder parts for 3D printing.*

3D PRINTING CHECKLISTS

Before Printing Your CAD

- See 3D Printing Basics on page 9 for printing tips.

- Use a raft or supports for the ball and the cradle mount due to the overhangs.

- Print the camera holder.

- After printing, remove any excess material with a file. Remove any rafts or supports.

Quality Control & Product Testing

- Test the product for its ability to mount and pivot a camera 360 degrees. Assemble as shown in fig. 8.

FIG. 8: *The assembled parts of the camera holder.*

THINK ABOUT IT

Consider these questions and make notes about possible answers. You can test them by modifying and printing a new version of your design.

What would happen if the difference between the diameter of the ball and the internal diameter of the socket were only 0.5 mm?

Why are there slots in the socket?

DESIGN CHALLENGE

Can you design a ball-and-socket joint that locks in place?

THE SCIENCE BEHIND IT

The roundness of the ball in a ball-and-socket joint ensures for a smooth pivot in all directions. This is essential when using it as a camera mount, which usually requires nonjerky movement, which for smooth video and pictures.

Lockable Ball-and-Socket Camera Holder

In Lab 15, we designed a camera holder using a ball-and-socket joint. The weight of the camera will pull the camera down unless it is perfectly upright. We will need to lock the camera in other positions against the force of gravity. In this project we create a locking mechanism for the ball-and-socket joint.

DESIGN NOTES

The design can vary greatly based on how many locking positions you want. We will limit our design to locking the camera holder in the vertical position. The parts you will make in addition to the parts from the design in Lab 15 are:

Key seat(s) in the ball
Key hole(s) in the socket
Key

THE DESIGN PROCESS

Creating the key seats

1. We start off by first lining up the slotted socket section and ball section from the previous Lab. Convert the socket material to **Transparent** (fig. 1, arrow 2) so you can ensure they are lined up correctly—that is, with an equal gap on all sides between the ball and the inside of the socket (fig. 1, arrow 1).

2. Separate the two sections but keep them at the same height and angles they were when lined up.

3. We will now create a keyhole so we can lock the holder in a vertical position. Create a 2 mm × 2 mm × 20 mm **Rectangular Box Hole**. Merge it with the socket at the about half the height of the socket (note the height from the workplane; see the arrow in fig. 2). **Group** the box hole with the socket to form the keyhole in the socket (fig. 3).

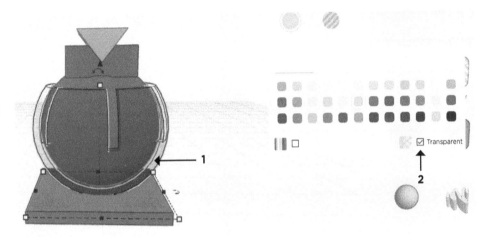

FIG. 1: *Convert the socket part of the ball joint to transparent.*

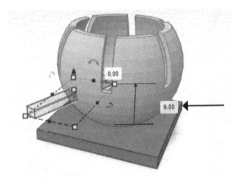

FIG. 2: *Create a box-shaped hole in the socket.*

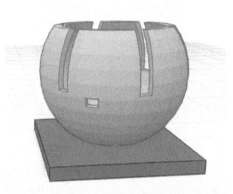

FIG. 3: *The completed box-shaped hole in the socket.*

4. Now we will create the key seat in the ball section so we can lock the holder in the vertical position. Make a copy of the rectangular box hole from step 2. Merge it with the ball at the same height from the workplane and same angle as you did in step 2 (fig. 4). Group the box hole with the ball section to create the key seat in the ball (fig. 5).

5. To create the key, simply create a trapezoid using the **Trapezoid** tool. The wider end should be 1.5 mm × 1.5 mm with a length of 10 mm (fig. 6).

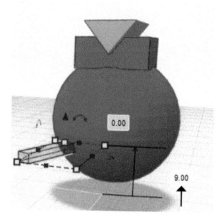

FIG. 4: *Create a matching box hole for the key seat in the ball section of the joint at the same height and angle as the hole in the socket section.*

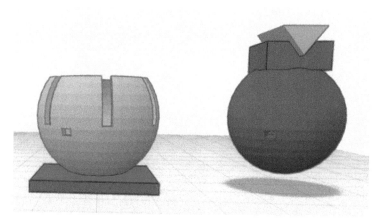

FIG. 5: *The completed key seat in the ball-and-socket joint.*

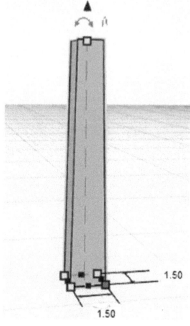

FIG. 6: *Create the key using a trapezoid.*

3D PRINTING CHECKLISTS

Before Printing Your CAD

- See 3D Printing Basics on page 9 for printing tips.

- Print the lockable camera holder.

- After printing, remove any excess material with a file. Remove any rafts or supports.

Quality Control & Product Testing

- Test the product for its ability to pivot and lock a camera into position at the vertical.

THINK ABOUT IT

Consider this question and make notes about possible answers. You can test them by modifying and printing a new version of your design.

What would happen if we made the key seat at the point of the slots in the socket section?

DESIGN CHALLENGE

Can you lock the camera in the vertical position without a key?

THE SCIENCE BEHIND IT

A key in a mechanical system can be used to transmit as well as restrict motion or torque. The gap where the key sits is called the key seat. The tolerances between the key, key seat, and mating parts in the mechanical system are critical in transmitting or restricting motion, and vary based on the material being used to print/manufacture the parts. Chamfers are sometimes used to improve functionality as they provide a wider mouth for the key to enter the keyhole without sacrificing the tight tolerances of the mating surfaces further in the hole.

3D Puzzles

In this Lab we use our knowledge of joints to create interlocking 3D puzzles. While most 2D puzzles don't have to be solved in any particular sequence, the solution for the 3D puzzle designed in this Lab must follow a particular sequence. When designing a puzzle we must first decide how many pieces there will be in the puzzle, and what sequence we want to follow.

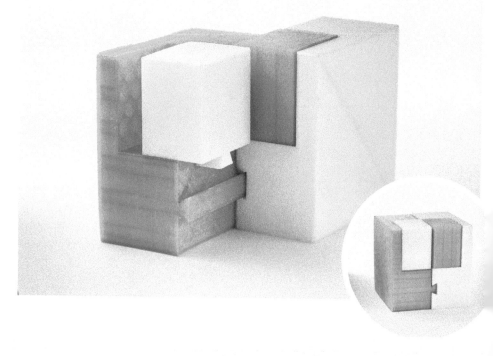

DESIGN NOTES

Our design will have four pieces that require two smaller pieces to attach to the larger pieces prior to joining the larger pieces together (fig. 1). We will use dovetail joints for this puzzle. The steps in the design will be:

Create the pieces
Identify the tails and sockets for each joint
Create the joints

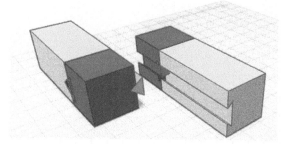

FIG. 1: *The smaller, red pieces slide onto the larger yellow pieces first. Then the two pieces slide together to create a multistep 3D puzzle.*

THE DESIGN PROCESS

1. We start by creating a 20 mm × 20 mm box. Make a copy of this box. We now have two small puzzle pieces.

2. Then make a 44 mm × 20 mm box and make a copy of it. We now have two larger puzzle pieces as well. Fig. 2 shows all four pieces.

3. Identify the mating surfaces. This is key so we can ensure each joint has matching tail and socket pieces (fig. 3).

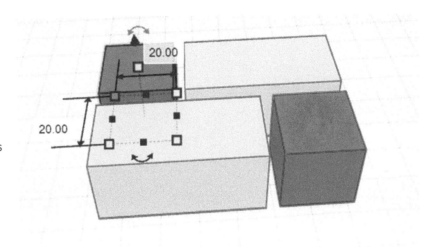

FIG. 2: *Create four boxes for the puzzle shapes.*

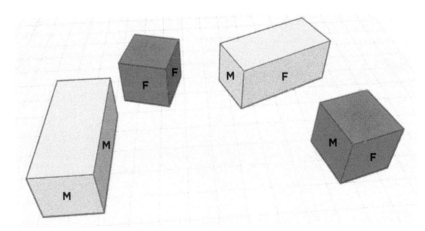

FIG. 3: *Identify which surfaces will be adjoining in the puzzle. The M and F surfaces adjacent in the figure will mate one another.*

4. Now create the dovetail joints for all pieces. Follow the steps in Lab 13 (page 72) to ensure good fits. Fig. 4 shows the dovetail joint for one big and one small piece of the puzzle. Fig. 5 shows all pieces with dovetail joints.

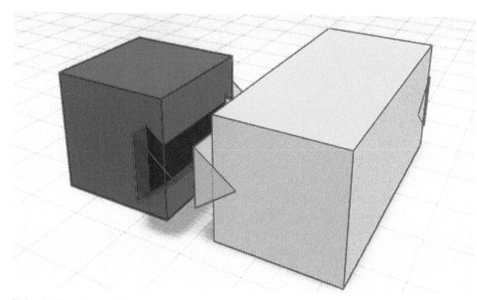

FIG. 4: *The dovetail joint on one larger and one smaller piece of the puzzle.*

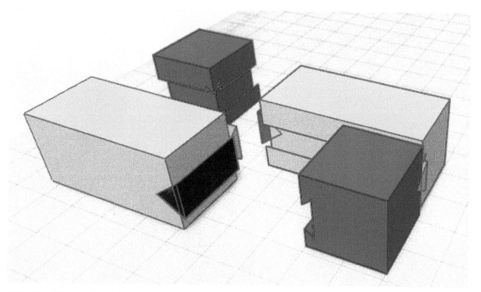

FIG. 5: *All puzzle pieces with the completed dovetail joints.*

3D PRINTING CHECKLISTS

Before Printing Your CAD

- See 3D Printing Basics on page 9 for printing tips.
- Print the puzzle.
- After printing, remove any excess material with a file.

Quality Control & Product Testing

- Test the product to see whether you can put the puzzle together.

THINK ABOUT IT

Consider these questions and make notes about possible answers. You can test them by modifying and printing a new version of your design.

Could you change the sequence of assembly? If not, how would you modify the design so you could?

DESIGN CHALLENGE

Can you use another dovetail joint to lock two puzzle pieces together that are not locked together directly now?

THE SCIENCE BEHIND IT

Throughout history, 3D puzzles have been used extensively to create lockable storage devices. They're featured in many historically inspired films (such as National Treasure) as well. Some 3D puzzles have puzzles built within them as a second level of security. Puzzles can also incorporate different types of joints.

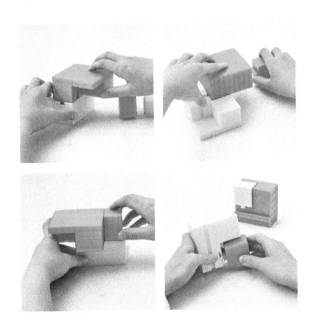

Body Part: Human Hand

In this Lab we will apply our skills in designing joints to model the palm and fingers of a human hand. An individual finger bone is called a phalanx. All the finger bones together are called phalanges. The fingers are connected to the palm by ellipsoid joints, but we will model them as ball-and-socket joints in this project because our joints won't be held together with ligaments. This time we will use ball-and-socket joint tools that are prebuilt in the Tinkercad software. The standard ball-and-socket joint tool in Tinkercad is slightly different from the one we designed in Lab 15 because it has only one slot.

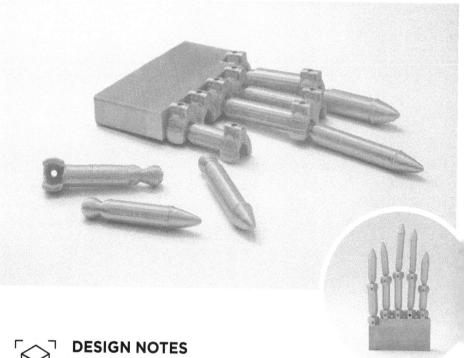

DESIGN NOTES

A basic human hand has the following parts, for the purpose of our design. Parts of the body are often labeled with a location tag in addition to their names. *Proximal* means closer to the center of the body. *Distal* means farther from the center of the body.

Palm
Knuckles (socket)
Ball and fingers (proximal phalanx)
Fingers (middle phalanx)
Fingertip (distal phalanx)

THE DESIGN PROCESS

1. Create the palm of the hand using two different **Box** tools. Create a palm of width 73 mm × 16 mm (fig. 1). The lower seat portion is the side of the thumb.

2. We will now use the **Socket** tool from the **Connector** toolbox to create the socket of the ball-and-socket joint of the knuckle (fig. 2 arrow identifies the socket tool). We will not resize the socket tool as it is matched to the ball tool for the rest of the joint.

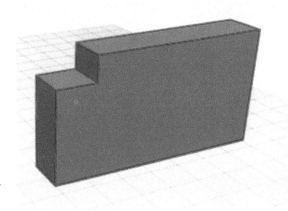

FIG. 1: *Use two boxes to create a model of a palm with the lower portion representing the thumb side.*

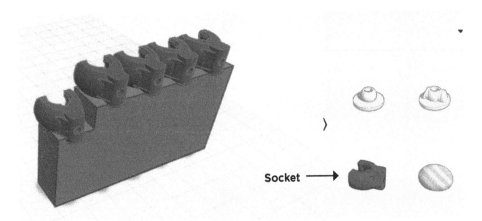

FIG. 2: *Add sockets for the knuckles.*

3. Create the ball and fingers (proximal phalanx) using the **Ball** tool from the **Connector** toolbox to create the ball of the ball-and-socket joint (fig. 3). We will not resize the ball tool as it is matched to the socket tool we created in step 2.

4. To create the fingers, use the **Cylinder** tool with proportionate lengths for each finger. Match length and width to those of your own finger (fig. 3).

5. Repeat steps 3 and 4 to create the rest of the fingers as shown in fig. 4. Add a knuckle (see step 2) to the other end of each finger as seen in fig. 4. The proximal phalanx will attach to this knuckle.

6. Create the middle phalanx by repeating steps 2–4 to create the middle phalanx and matching ball of the knuckle (fig. 5, #1).

7. Add the fingertip using the **Paraboloid** tool as shown in fig. 5, arrow 2. Repeat step 5 and 6 for all fingers.

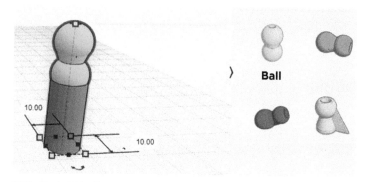

FIG. 3: *Add balls to cylinders to create fingers.*

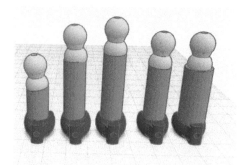

FIG. 4: *Add sockets for the knuckle joints to the finger at the opposite end from the ball joints.*

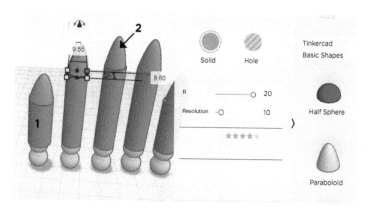

FIG. 5: *Add a fingertip to each finger.*

3D PRINTING CHECKLISTS

Before Printing Your CAD

- See 3D Printing Basics on page 9 for printing tips.

- Print the hand.

- After printing, remove any excess material with a file.

Quality Control & Product Testing

- Assemble all the knuckles by putting balls into sockets (fig. 6).

- Test the product for its ability to curve its fingers.

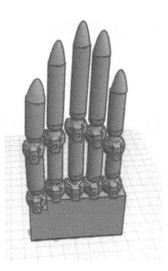

FIG. 6: *The CAD view of the assembled hand with fingers and palm.*

DESIGN CHALLENGE

Can you design the fingertip with a ball-and-socket joint as well?

THE SCIENCE BEHIND IT

The human hand has 14 bones and 14 joints in the fingers alone. The joints allow for flexion and extension and some rotational and side-to-side movement—but only at the connection of the fingers to the palm. The rotational motion of the hand comes primarily from the wrist. Humans have opposable thumbs, which allows us to have a variety of grips that can range from holding a delicate glass, to writing, to climbing and grabbing. The opposable thumb is key to a lot of dexterity, which also exists for some other primates. Some animals have opposable big toes.

THINK ABOUT IT

Consider this question and make notes about possible answers. You can test them by modifying and printing a new version of your design.

How would using the ball-and-socket joint designed in Lab 15 change how the finger moves?

Body System: Human Arm

For this Lab we will extend our design skills of complex human body parts to design a human arm. Our model is simplified with only one forearm bone instead of two, and with the hand as one single piece.

DESIGN NOTES

For the purpose of our design, a basic human arm has the following parts:

Shoulder joint
Upper arm
Elbow joint
Forearm (with a single bone)
Wrist joint
Hand (as a single piece without joints)

THE DESIGN PROCESS

1. Create the shoulder joint. The shoulder joint is modeled using the ball-and-socket joint we created in Lab 15 (page 80). The socket inner diameter is 23 mm and the ball is 22 mm diameter in fig. 1.

2. We will model the upper arm as a tapered tubular shape. We used the **High Resolution Tube** shape generator tool. See fig. 2, arrow 1 for details and dimensions.

3. The elbow joint can be modeled using the same ball-and-socket joint we used for the shoulder joint in step 1. We can simply make a copy of it and resize to fit the smaller end of the upper arm as shown in fig. 1. The inner diameter of the elbow joint socket is 18 mm. The diameter of the elbow joint ball is 17 mm.

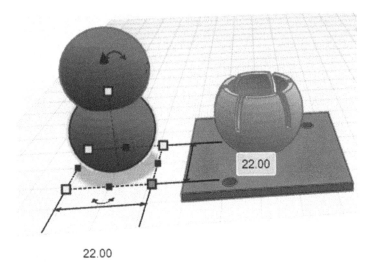

FIG. 1: *Create a model of the shoulder using a ball-and-socket joint.*

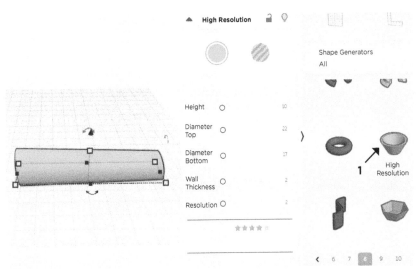

FIG. 2: *Make the upper arm using a* **High Resolution Tube**.

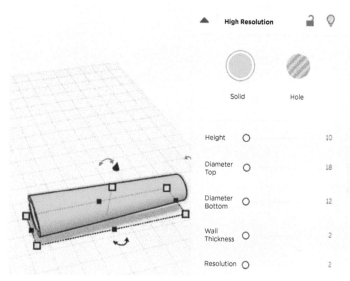

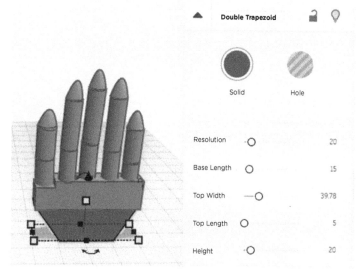

High Resolution		
Solid		Hole
Height	○	10
Diameter Top	○	18
Diameter Bottom	○	12
Wall Thickness	○	2
Resolution	○	2

Double Trapezoid		
Solid		Hole
Resolution	○	20
Base Length	○	15
Top Width	─○	39.78
Top Length	○	5
Height	○	20

FIG. 3: *Copy the upper arm and resize it to create the forearm.*

FIG. 4: *Make a simple hand form with no joints.*

4. The forearm is modeled using the same tool as the upper arm (fig. 3). The dimensions of the larger end must match the dimensions of the ball in the elbow joint.

5. The wrist can be modeled using the ball-and-socket joint as well. Socket dimensions must match the narrower end of the forearm.

6. The hand connects to the wrist using the wrist joint. The hand shown in fig. 4 is modeled after the hand in Lab 18 (page 94), but as a single piece without joints.

7. Prior to printing, we will need to reposition some of the parts. The sockets of each joint attach to the part above it, and the ball attaches to the part following it in the sequence of parts of the arm. See fig. 5 for the print layout.

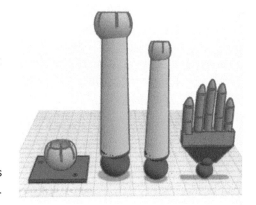

FIG. 5: *The positioning of parts for 3D printing.*

3D PRINTING CHECKLISTS

Before Printing Your CAD

- See 3D Printing Basics on page 9 for printing tips.

- Print the arm.

- After printing, remove any excess material with a file. Remove any rafts or supports.

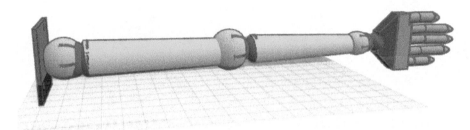

FIG. 6: *A CAD Image showing the assembled arm with joints.*

Quality Control & Product Testing

- Assemble all the parts (fig. 6). Test the product for its range of motion.

THINK ABOUT IT

Consider this question and make notes about possible answers. You can test them by modifying and printing a new version of your design.

How would using the ball-and-socket joint designed in Lab 18 for the knuckles change how the shoulder moves?

DESIGN CHALLENGE

Can you design the elbow joint to restrict extension to 180 degrees, so it more closely matches a real human elbow?

THE SCIENCE BEHIND IT

The human arm uses a series of joints in the shoulder, elbow, and wrist to allow for an extensive range of motion that can be controlled in small increments along all three axes of linear motion in addition to rotational motion.

The arm is used to signify various meanings in different cultures. In Hinduism, some of the gods have multiple arms to signify omnipotence. Raising arms above the shoulder signify capitulation or surrender during conflict. A single raised arm signifies presence during roll call. Arm motions are important in directing traffic.

LAB 20

Mini Guitars with Multiple String Types

In this Lab we learn how various materials can interact with the same structure to produce different sound. We will design a mini-guitar and test the sound using different materials for the guitar strings.

DESIGN NOTES

For the purpose of our design, a basic mini-guitar has the following parts:

Body

Sound Hole

Neck with Frets and Headstock

Bridge

String Conduit

Strings (non-designed, non-3D printed)

THE DESIGN PROCESS

Creating the body

1. The guitar body is a nonbasic shape and is hard to model using a composite of basic shapes. We will use the **Scribble** tool from the **Basic Shapes** toolbox to design the guitar body. Fig. 1 shows how to use the **Scribble** tool to design a rough 3D solid guitar body. Arrow 1 in the image identifies the tool to use.

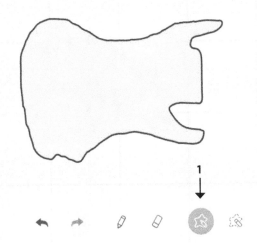

FIG. 1: *Use the* **Scribble** *tool to design the guitar body.*

2. The body created in step 1 looks rough. It is smoothed out using the **Erase** tool as shown in fig. 2. Arrow 1 in the image identifies the **Erase** tool, and arrow 2 shows how it is applied to smooth the edge of the guitar body. Click the **Done** button to complete editing the shape. Fig. 3 shows the resulting 3D guitar body after initial smoothing of the body. Keep editing the body by smoothing the edges to get the desired shape of the guitar body. Fig. 4 shows a comparison between initial smoothing and final guitar body.

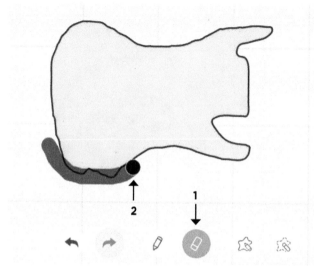

FIG. 2: *Use the erase function to smooth out the scribble.*

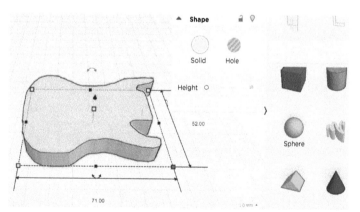

FIG. 3: *The guitar body shape after initial smoothing.*

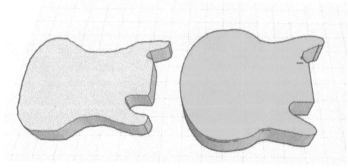

FIG. 4: *The comparison between the initial guitar shape and final shape after smoothing is complete.*

3. The sound hole is created by making a cylindrical hole in the center of the top face of the guitar body. The hole must be 2 mm from the bottom surface of the guitar. See fig. 5 for sound hole dimensions and location.

4. The guitar body is currently a solid object with a hole in the center. However, to improve the sound quality it needs |to be hollowed out. We will use a **New Banana** tool from the **Shape Generator—All** toolbox. This shape when converted to a hole (instead of solid) helps to hollow out the guitar body while minimizing overhangs for the 3D-printing process. Fig. 6 shows the new banana hole shape embedded in the transparent guitar body. Ensure that the top and bottom faces of the guitar body are always 2 mm thick, except at the point of the sound hole.

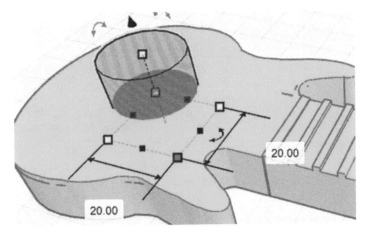

FIG. 5: *Make the sound hole in the guitar body.*

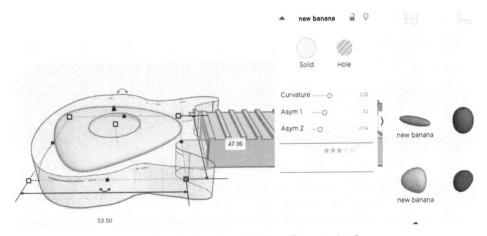

FIG. 6: *Hollow out the guitar body using the **New Banana** tool.*

5. The neck and frets with headstock are composed of a series of basic shapes. Frets should not be more than 2 mm thick. See fig. 7 for a sample design.

6. The bridge raises the guitar strings off the guitar body so they can vibrate freely to produce clear sound. The bridge is created using basic box shapes (fig. 8). Take care to align the bridge to the corresponding bridge on the headstock of the guitar (fig. 8, arrow 1).

7. The string conduit guides the string along the back of the guitar where it can be fastened. The ridges along the side of the guitar body in fig. 8, arrow 2 and the ridges on the back of the guitar body in fig. 9 show an example of the conduit design. Take care to ensure the guitar body always has a 2 mm thickness at all points, except the sound hole on the top center.

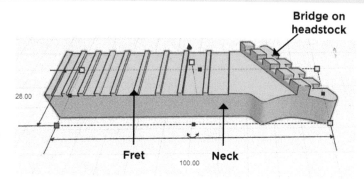

FIG. 7: *Create the guitar neck, frets, and headstock using basic shapes.*

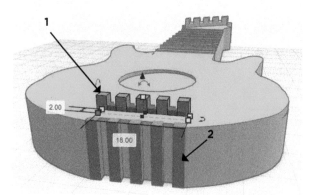

FIG. 8: *Use boxes to create a bridge and the guitar string conduits.*

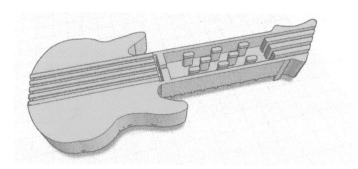

FIG. 9: *The back of the guitar showing the grooves for the string.*

3D PRINTING CHECKLISTS

Before Printing Your CAD

- See 3D Printing Basics on page 9 for printing tips.

- Print the guitar.

- After printing, remove any excess material with a file. Remove any rafts or supports.

Quality Control & Product Testing

- Assemble the guitar using rubber bands as strings (fig. 9). Test the product for sound using plastic and rubber bands. Also, test the sound using string, actual guitar wire, and copper wire. Note the difference.

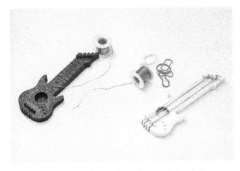

FIG. 10: *3D-printed guitar with strings assembled.*

DESIGN CHALLENGE

How would you modify the sound hole to increase the volume?

THE SCIENCE BEHIND IT

Guitars are commonly used musical instruments that fall into the string instruments category. A string instrument produces sound by vibrating when struck. The vibration is amplified using a sound hole. The amount of sound produced by the sound hole is a function of the perimeter of the sound hole rather than the area of the sound hole.

THINK ABOUT IT

Consider these questions and make notes about possible answers. You can test them by modifying and printing a new version of your design.

Why did we use the New Banana tool instead of a basic shape tool to hollow out the guitar?

Reverse Engineering

Sometimes we come across objects that are extremely well designed and that we may want to replicate. However, they may have parts that are concealed, so the design is not immediately apparent.

In such cases, we have to reverse the manufacturing process: disassemble, measure, sketch, and model in CAD. This process is called reverse-engineering. Typically, you want to pick objects with fewer than 15 pieces to reverse-engineer. In this lab we reverse-engineer a mechanically operated, retractable writing pen that has seven parts to it. We will use off-the-shelf refills for ink.

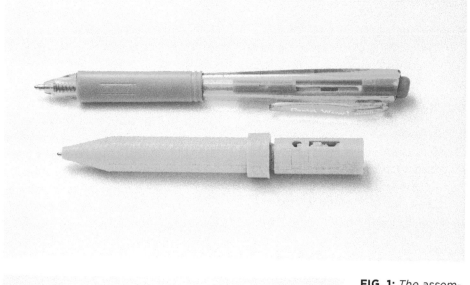

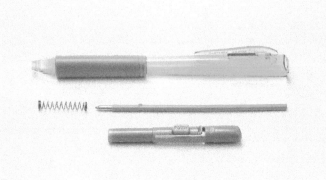

FIG. 1: *The assembled and disassembled views of a pen accompanied by an assembled view of a 3D-printed pen for comparison.*

DESIGN NOTES

A basic, mechanically operated, retractable writing pen has the following parts, for the purpose of our design:

Body casing
Head casing
Refill and spring (purchased separately)
Inner tube
On-off button/actuator
On-off button to refill connector
Body-head casing fastener
Pen clip (optional)

Sketch the different parts above based on the disassembled pen; try to approximate the drawing to basic shapes (cubes, cylinders, etc.)

THE DESIGN PROCESS

Creating the body casing

1. As a first step in reverse engineering, we need to disassemble the product. Fig. 1 shows the disassembled parts of the pen. Measure the different parts.

2. We will model using basic 3D elements to represent shapes. The body casing looks like a hollow cylinder that tapers on one end. We will model it as the combination of a regular hollow **Cylinder** (fig. 2, arrow 1) and a regular hollow **Cone** that is snipped on the narrow end (fig. 2, arrow 2). The cone is snipped on one end to allow for the refill to exit the casing. The hole in the cone tip must be 2.5 mm (or slightly larger than the diameter of the refill you will be using). Total body-casing length about 76 mm, but will vary depending on the ink refill used.

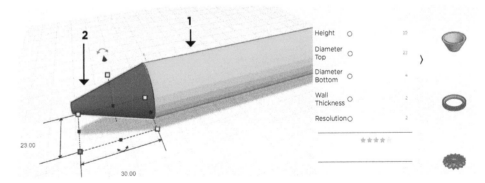

FIG. 2: *Make the body casing by joining a cylinder and a snipped cone.*

Creating the head casing

3. The head casing can be modeled as a regular hollow **Cylinder** that is open on one end. The diameter of cylinder should be the same as that of the body casing cylinder (fig. 3). The head casing will also have two holes for the on-off buttons to extend through, as identified by arrow 1 in fig. 3. The length of the head casing is 32 mm.

4. The button is the point of interaction between the user and the pen. When pushed down, it pushes the refill out of the casing. When pushed up, the refill retracts into the casing.

5. The button is mounted on an inner tube that slides in the head casing. This inner tube is 1 mm smaller than the inner diameter of the head casing and about 25 mm long. We add two notches to it spaced 5 mm apart; this forms a thin strip called button strip. In fig. 4, arrow 1 identifies the notches, and arrow 2 identifies the resetting button strip. The height of the inner tube is about 5 mm taller than that of the head casing.

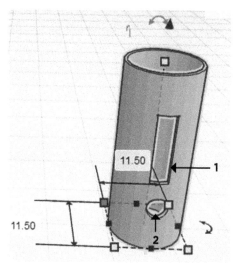

FIG. 3: *Make a head casing with a slot and a round hole.*

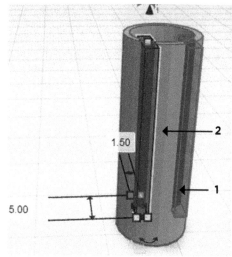

FIG. 4: *Make an inner tube with notches and a button strip.*

6. Next, we add the button and the lock to the button strip to create the on-off button/actuator. The push button is 2 mm × 2 mm. The lock is a sphere, 2mm in diameter. The dimensions of the button and lock should be smaller than the corresponding holes on the head casing. In fig. 5, arrow 1 identifies the lock and arrow 2 identifies the on/off button.

7. The button strip has to flex with each press of the button. This feature is added to the button strip by separating it from the inner tube and then reattaching it to the tube using the **S-wall** tool (which mimics a spring). One end of the **S-wall** tool connects to the base of the inner tube and the other connects to the button strip. The height should be set so the buttons will line up with the holes on the head casing. Fig. 6 shows a transparent inner tube, so we can easily see the **S-wall** tool. Arrow 1 shows where to find the tool, and arrow 2 shows the location and orientation of the tool in the design.

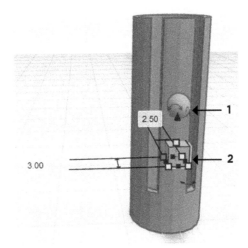

FIG. 5: *Add a button and a lock to the button strip.*

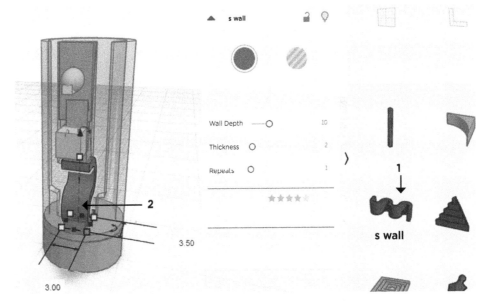

FIG. 6: *Add an S-wall to serve as a spring for the button strip.*

Creating the fasten or connecting the head casing to the body casing

8. The head casing is fastened to the body casing using a screw-on method. The **ISO Metric Thread** tool can be used to create the bolt for the head casing. Also insert a **Hole** through the center of the bolt for the refill to pass through. The hole should be 3.5 mm (depends on the diameter of the refill). Fig. 7 shows a transparent head casing so we can view the ISO metric thread and through hole.

9. We will also need to make the corresponding nut in the body casing for the bolt to screw into. To create the nut we create a hole (in the shape of the iso metric thread tool) in a cylinder about the same diameter as the body casing. Note that the diameter of the Iso Metric Thread tool for the nut must be 0.5 mm more than the diameter of the Iso Metric Thread tool for the bolt for smooth mating of the nut and bolt. Fig. 8 shows the creation of the nut in arrow 1, and the nut mounted on the body casing in arrow 2.

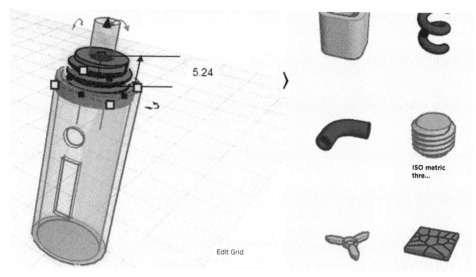

FIG. 7: *Add a bolt and a hole to the head casing.*

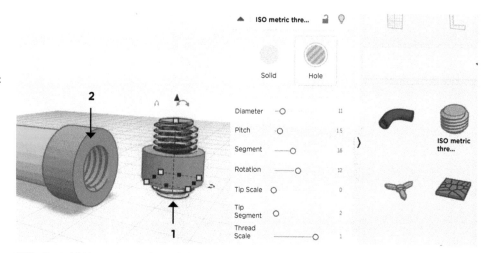

FIG. 8: *Add the nut portion of the fastener to the body casing.*

3D PRINTING CHECKLISTS

Before Printing Your CAD

- See 3D Printing Basics on page 9 for printing tips.

- Print the pen.

- After printing, remove any excess material with a file.

Quality Control & Product Testing

- Assemble the inner tube into the head casing and fasten it to the body casing after inserting the refill and the spring.

- Twist and lock the casings into place.

- Push the **On/Off** button to push the refill out of the casing and push it back to retract the refill tip. See fig. 9 for exploded view of assembly sequence.

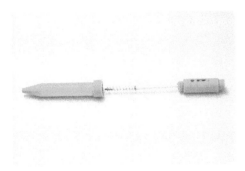

FIG. 9: *The assembly sequence of 3D-printed pen parts.*

DESIGN CHALLENGE

Can you design a clip for the pen so it can be attached to a shirt pocket?

THE SCIENCE BEHIND IT

Retractable pens have been in existence for over 50 years. The more common retractable pens nowadays are click pens. They operate using a special cam mechanism that converts translational motion into rotational motion. These can also be designed using the reverse-engineering process.

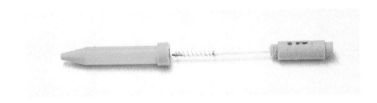

THINK ABOUT IT

Consider this question and make notes about possible answers. You can test them by modifying and printing a new version of your design.

What would happen if we swapped the positions of the button and lock in step 6?

LAB 22

Thingiverse: Downloadable 3D Models

We reverse engineered a retractable pen in the previous Lab. We saw that there were many parts to design and the button mechanism was a bit sticky. In Lab 17, we designed a 3D puzzle that also required tight tolerances on the dovetail joints. In such cases, it may be more efficient to use models that have been predesigned by someone else that meet our specifications. There are a couple online websites that provide warehouses of exactly such designs. Thingiverse is one such website.

DESIGN NOTES

The basic process to design by legally using someone else's design files from sites like Thingiverse is:

1. Search and locate the completed design to emulate
2. Download the files to your computer
3. Upload the files from your computer to Tinkercad
4. Edit the files in Tinkercad to your specifications
5. Print the edited files

For this Lab we will aim to use a design from Thingiverse as a jumping-off point for our 3D puzzle project.

THE DESIGN PROCESS

1. Link to Thingiverse:
   https://www.Thingiverse.com/

2. Search and locate a completed design
   to emulate. Go to the Thingiverse
   website and search for 3D Puzzles.

3. After selecting the desired design, click
   on it to access the files to download.
   We used "Printable Interlocking Puzzle."
   Inspect the design thoroughly prior to
   downloading to ensure it matches your
   requirements.

4. Open Tinkercad and click on **Create
   New Design** to get to a page with a
   blank workplane. Use the **Import Tool**,
   identified by the arrow in fig. 1, to
   import the completed design file onto
   the workplane. Repeat for all files you
   need to import.

5. Make any edits you desire. We edited
   the puzzle pieces to half their original
   size (fig. 2).

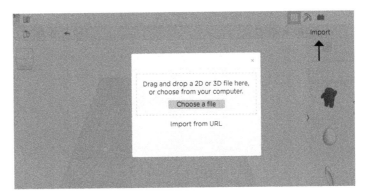

FIG. 1: *Import design files into Tinkercad.*

FIG. 2: *The edited puzzle pieces are half the size of
the originals.*

3D MARKETPLACES

In addition to Thingiverse, you can explore other online 3D marketplaces, where you can buy and sell downloadable files to 3D-print products and solutions to design problems. Some 3D marketplaces also offer other services, such as design software, online communities, and free download-able files.

Here's a list of some online 3D marketplaces.

3DExport

Clara.io

CGTrader

GradCAD

MyMiniFactory

Pinshape

Sculpteo

Shapeways

Turbosquid

Yeggi

Be sure to get your parents' permission before visiting these sites, signing up for a membership or subscription, or purchasing any products.

3D PRINTING CHECKLISTS

Before Printing Your CAD

- See 3D Printing Basics on page 9 for printing tips.

- Print the puzzle.

- After printing, remove any excess material with a file. Remove any rafts or supports.

Quality Control & Product Testing

- Assemble the puzzle pieces together.

DESIGN CHALLENGE

Can you find a 3D-printable puzzle to modify where the sequence of assembly does not matter?

DESIGN CHALLENGE

Using work from other designers is an efficient way to build your design skills. It is ethical and courteous to credit and/or cite the creator of the original design. Some designs are not available for download while others are available for download, either for free or a fee.

MAKING 3D PROJECTS WITH SKETCHUP

In this unit, we learn the basics of SketchUp, a free, easy-to-use online program for designing objects for 3D printing. The program will help us develop our skills to design and create objects using discrete basic elements for shapes. We will create some projects, building on what we learn in each Lab to create objects that are increasingly complex and parallel to the design from the Tinkercad software projects. Let's get making!

GETTING STARTED WITH SKETCHUP

SketchUp is computer-aided design (CAD) software used to create digital models in 3D by using its library of precreated 2D shapes and shape elements. Options exist for student versions as well, at a heavily discounted price. Once you have installed the software and launched it, you will be prompted by the software with a screen similar to the one in fig. 1. Click the **Start Using SketchUp** or **Start Modeling** button to proceed.

This will bring you to the window where you will create your designs (fig. 1). If prompted with a request to select the units of measurement for your design page, select millimeters (mm) or inches (in.). You can modify this later depending on the design project you are working on. The design window has the following parts that are used for different purposes.

Top Ribbon has multiple drop-down menus—**File**, **Edit**, **View**, **Draw**, **Tools**. Click on each one of them to view the options. The **File** dropdown is key to save your designs and to export them for printing. The **Edit** drop-down has the important **Undo** function.

Design Icon Ribbon This ribbon, right below the top ribbon, has various icons that are used to create your designs. Hover over them with your mouse to see what each of them can do. Fig. 1 shows the **Select** tool.

Central Design Area The entire area, with the axes and the man, is your primary design workspace. The man can be deleted by simply clicking on him and hitting the delete button on your keyboard. The axes are added as a guide and can also be removed it desired.

Right Pane The right pane is key to providing support during the design stage and for additional options. Fig. 2 identifies the right pane. Click on any dropdown button—**Materials**, **Instructor**, **Entity Info**—to learn more about it. The Instructor feature is key as it provides a detailed visual animation on how to use each of the tools in the Design Icon ribbon.

Bottom Pane The pane at the bottom gives further directions on using the design tools/icons. It also gives the measurements of the objects drawn in the workspace. Fig. 3 (see next page) shows the measurements of one of the rectangles drawn as well as the directions to draw the rectangles in the bottom pane and the right pane.

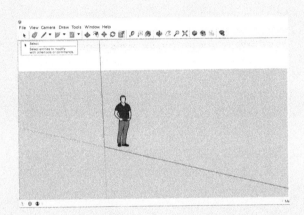

FIG. 1: *The Select tool in the Design Icon Ribbon in SketchUp.*

FIG. 2: *The Right Pane in the SketchUp window provides user support for various tools.*

Triggers Once you draw a shape or element in SketchUp, you can add other shapes or elements relative to the original shape or relative to the workspace. Fig. 4 shows a shape being added relative to the endpoint of the previous shape. A shape can also be added to the midpoint of another shape (fig. 5). Shapes can be added from an edge (fig. 6) or a face (fig. 7) or from any point on the shape or axis.

Exporting STL files from SketchUp – Most 3D printers will accept files in a specific .STL format. In SketchUp, you will need to download an extension software from the Extension Warehouse to convert your designs into .STL format. Fig. 8 shows how to get to the Extension Warehouse.

Note that, unlike in Tinkercad, where you can right-click and drag to change the view, in SketchUp you have to use the tools in the icon ribbon to change the view—**Pan** and **Zoom**. There are other tools and tips in SketchUp that will grow your skills in computer-aided design, some of which will be discussed in the Labs in this unit. Continue to explore yourself for different/easier ways to navigate the software.

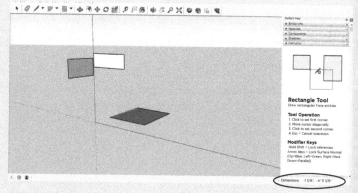

FIG. 3: *The measurement of the shape in the Bottom Pane.*

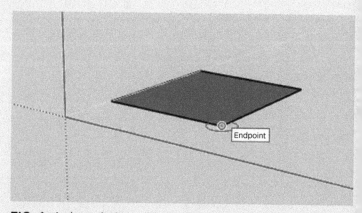

FIG. 4: *A shape being added relative to the endpoint of the previous shape.*

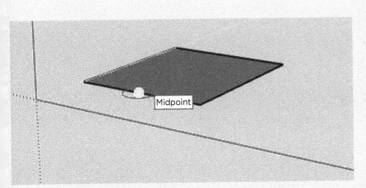

FIG. 5: *The shape being added to the midpoint of another shape.*

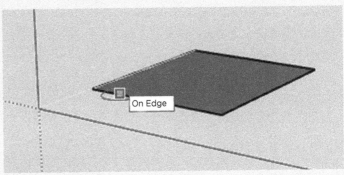

FIG. 6: *A shape being added to the edge of another shape.*

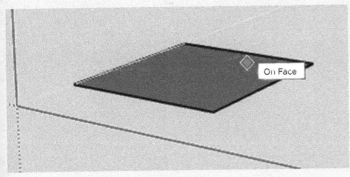

FIG. 7: *A shape being added to the face of another shape.*

FIG. 8: *How to navigate to the* **Extension Warehouse** *in SketchUp.*

LAB 23

Basic 3D Shapes

In this Lab we learn how to use SketchUp to create basic 3D shapes. Unlike Tinkercad, which offers a toolbox of precreated 3D shapes, SketchUp offers a toolbox of 2D shapes. We can use these 2D shapes to create 3D shapes by extruding them—stretching them out in a specific direction.

THE DESIGN PROCESS

Creating a basic box/rectangular prism and cylinder:

1. Select the **Rectangle** tool from the Ribbon at the top of the screen. Then click and drag your cursor to create a rectangle of dimensions small enough to view on the screen (fig. 1). You can draw the rectangle anywhere on the work area.

2. Now select the **Push/Pull** tool from the Ribbon (fig. 2). Point it at the top face of the 2D rectangle (fig. 2) and drag to the desired height (about an inch, or 25 mm). Feel free to readjust the height using the Push/Pull tool to give you a feel for the tool.

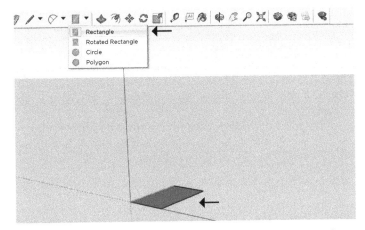

FIG. 1: *Draw a rectangle by selecting the **Rectangle** tool from the menu.*

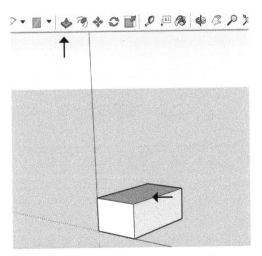

FIG. 2: *Stretch the rectangle using the* **Push/Pull** *tool.*

3. You can use the **Tape Measure** tool to measure the dimensions of the 3D shape (fig. 3). The **Text** tool to the right of the Tape Measure tool will let you label your measurements by simply selecting it and then clicking on the desired edge to be measured.

4. Now, to create a cylinder. Similar to step 1 above, select the **Circle** tool (fig. 4) and draw a circle so it lies flat on the workspace. Note that the outline of the circle will change color to match the axis it corresponds to.

5. Follow step 2 to extrude the circle to convert it to a cylinder (fig. 5).

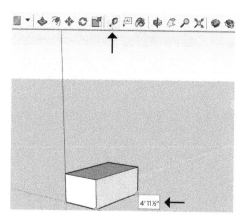

FIG. 3: *Use the* **Tape Measure** *tool to find the dimensions of the shape. Add a label with the* **Text** *tool.*

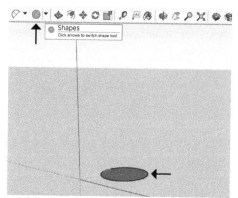

FIG. 4: *Add a circle to the workspace using the* **Circle** *tool.*

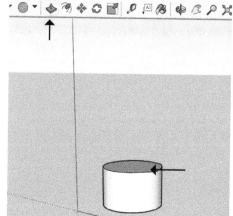

FIG. 5: *Stretch the circle into a cylinder.*

3D PRINTING CHECKLISTS

Before Printing Your CAD

- See 3D Printing Basics on page 9 for printing tips.

- Print the cylinder.

- After printing, remove any excess material with a file.

Quality Control & Product Testing

- Inspect the printed object for the individual layers of plastic filament.

THINK ABOUT IT

Consider these questions and make notes about possible answers. You can test them by modifying and printing a new version of your design.

What was the procedural difference in designing in Tinkercad versus SketchUp?

Which one was easier to learn and why?

DESIGN CHALLENGE

Can you create a pentagon-shaped prism using the tools in SketchUp?

THE SCIENCE BEHIND IT

Extrusion is a common manufacturing process for metals. The process begins with a metal sheet of fixed thickness. This sheet is then pushed into a mold of preset dimensions. This thins out the thickness of the sheet. The process is repeated multiple times until the desired thickness and shape of the final product are reached. Extrusion is a very efficient process for making metal products, such as cans, that are manufactured in high volume with consistent measurements. In SketchUp we model extrusion using the Push/Pull tool, but the thickness of the initial material does not decrease as we extrude it.

Removing Material from a 3D Object

LAB 24

In this Lab we learn how to use SketchUp to create basic holes in 3D shapes. Unlike in Tinkercad, which offers a hole tool, in SketchUp we have to use the Push/Pull tool to literally push a hole into a 3D shape.

DESIGN NOTES

Create a basic napkin ring in SketchUp by pushing a hole through a cylinder.

THE DESIGN PROCESS

1. Draw a cylinder in SketchUp with a diameter of about 2 inches, similar to Lab 23 (page 124). Arrow 1 in fig. 1 shows the initial circle drawn using the **Circle** tool, and arrow 2 shows the circle extruded into a cylinder using the **Push/Pull** tool.

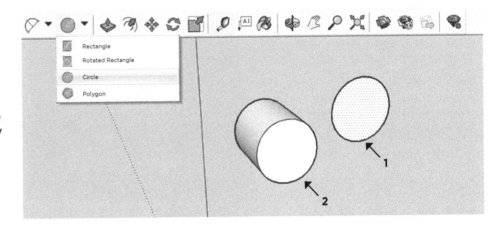

FIG. 1: *Create a cylinder.*

2. We now draw another circle on the
   front face of the cylinder. The size of
   the second circle is slightly smaller than
   that of the cylinder 1; this will determine
   the size of the hole in the napkin ring.
   Arrow 1 in fig. 2 shows the circle for the
   hole. Arrow 2 shows it being pushed
   back into the cylinder to the bottom
   edge of the cylinder. Note that if you do
   not push it to the edge, the material will
   get pushed in the opposite direction to
   form another cylinder.

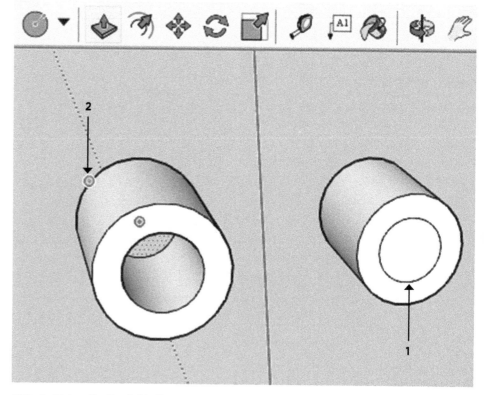

FIG. 2: *Using the* **Push/Pull** *tool to draw a circular hole in SketchUp.*

3D PRINTING CHECKLISTS

Before Printing Your CAD

- See 3D Printing Basics on page 9 for printing tips.

- Ensure the bottom surface of the prism and cylinder are touching the workplane/printing bed.

- Move the designs to the center of the workplane without them touching each other.

- Print the napkin ring.

- After printing, remove any excess material with a file.

Quality Control & Product Testing

- Test the napkin ring to see whether it will hold a napkin.

THINK ABOUT IT

Consider this question and make notes about possible answers. You can test them by modifying and printing a new version of your design.

What happens if you extend the push of the hole past the bottom edge of the cylinder?

DESIGN CHALLENGE

Can you create a blind hole (a hole that does not go all the way through) in a rectangular prism using SketchUp?

CONSIDERING CULTURE

Napkin rings are used to hold a folded napkin together. Early napkins were a third the size of the tablecloth and hence needed to be folded. Napkins are much smaller nowadays, and napkin rings are mostly ornamental. Napkins are folded into elaborate shapes and designs, but it was considered inappropriate to fold a napkin such that the pointy tip points to a monarch because it may signal assassination.

Removing Material and Combining Basic Shapes

In this Lab we extend our basic shape-making knowledge of SketchUp to making composite shapes to design menu holders. Restaurants often have specials that are listed on a single sheet of paper. A menu holder needs to be able to grip the paper as well as to keep the menu from flopping over. One way to keep a single sheet of paper from flopping over is to bend it or give it some curvature, which increases its rigidity.

DESIGN NOTES

A basic menu holder has the following parts:

Base

Curved walls (to grip menu)

THE DESIGN PROCESS

1. The base of the menu holder is simply a narrow rectangular strip that is no more than 2 mm thick. The length should be more than 50 mm (fig. 1).

2. Designing the curved walls by creating a cylinder using the process in Lab 23 (page 124). Draw a circle with center on the circumference that almost covers the cylinder completely (fig. 2).

3. Use the **Push/Pull** tool to extrude the overlapping circle to make another cylinder of the same thickness as the first cylinder (fig. 3).

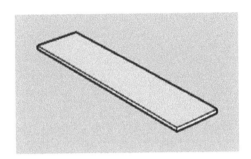

FIG. 1: *Create the base of the menu holder from a rectangular strip.*

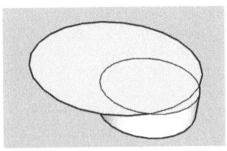

FIG. 2: *Make a cylinder and add a cutting circle.*

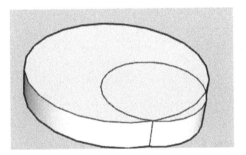

FIG. 3: *Make the cutting circle into a cylinder.*

4. Use the **Erase** tool to erase all the faces and lines except the small portion that will be the wall of the menu holder (fig. 4).

5. Make a copy of the wall by using the **Copy-Paste** tool in the **Edit** menu. Place the copy 2 mm away from the original. See fig. 5 for how to align the two walls.

6. Merge the base with the walls to complete the menu holder design (fig 6).

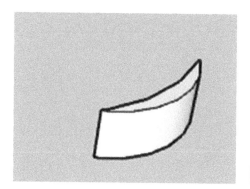

FIG. 4: *Erase everything except the crescent shape that will be one of the walls for the menu holder.*

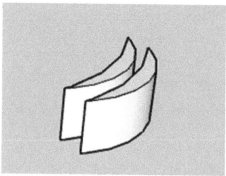

FIG. 5: *Copy the crescent shape and align to form the two walls of the holder.*

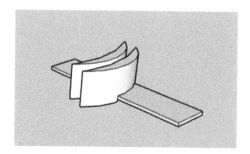

FIG. 6: *Merge the base with the walls.*

3D PRINTING CHECKLISTS

Before Printing Your CAD

- See 3D Printing Basics on page 9 for printing tips.

- Ensure the bottom surface of the base is touching the workplane/printing bed.

- Move the designs to the center of the workplane without them touching each other.

- Print the menu holder.

- After printing, remove any excess material with a file.

Quality Control & Product Testing

- Test the menu holder to see whether it can hold a sheet of paper without the paper flopping.

THINK ABOUT IT

Consider these questions and make notes about possible answers. You can test them by modifying and printing a new version of your design.

Would this menu holder help to keep any length paper upright? Why, or why not?

DESIGN CHALLENGE

Can you design a menu holder with noncurved walls?

THE SCIENCE BEHIND IT

The key to increasing the structural rigidity of a material is to increase the folds in it. By curving the paper of the menu, we are increasing its structural rigidity, thereby making it easier for it to stay upright. Another option for increasing the paper's rigidity is to fold it into an accordion shape; the triangles formed by the pleated folds increase its rigidity, while also making it harder to read the text that may have been printed on it.

Rear Wing for a Sports Car

Wings allow for a change in air flow on either side of them. In airplanes wings are angled so as to permit the plane to take off by gaining lift. However, in cars it is opposite. We want the car to stay in contact with the road even at higher speeds. We will design a wing for an automobile to exert downward pressure on it. The wing on a car is also called a spoiler.

THE DESIGN PROCESS

1. Use the **3D Warehouse** tool in SketchUp to find a good model for a car. Import that model onto the SketchUp work-plane (fig. 1).

2. Design the wing for the model by using the **Line** tool to draw the rear wing bracket (fig. 2).

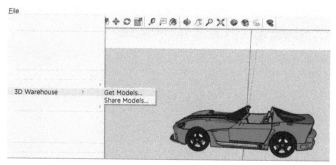

FIG. 1: *Find a pre-created design in the 3D warehouse.*

3. Extrude out the bracket and make a copy of it. Move them so they are about 50 mm apart, but not more apart than the width of the car (fig. 3).

4. Use the **Rectangle** tool to draw a rectangular wing that connects the top edges of the two brackets. Extrude out the rectangle to about 2 mm thickness (fig. 4).

5. Move the rear wing and brackets together to the rear of the car as seen in fig. 5.

6. Optional: Test the efficiency of the wing design in keeping downforce on the car. Download a copy of the .STL file and load it into the Autodesk Flow Design software, which will simulate liquid/ air flowing through the design. Adjust the source of the flow to line up with car wing. Start the flow simulation and observe how the flow changes due to the wing. Look for blue streaks; this indicates that air flow is slower at that point. We want slower air at the top of the wing to maximize downforce (fig. 6).

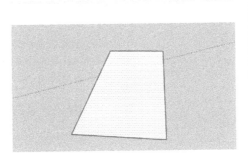

FIG. 2: *Draw a bracket for the wing.*

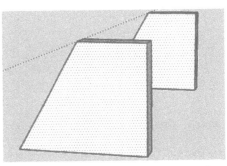

FIG. 3: *Extrude the wing bracket to the desired thickness.*

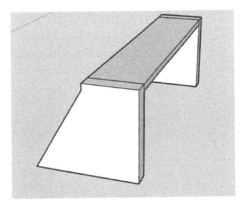

FIG. 4: *Design the wing.*

FIG. 5: *Merge the wing and brackets and move to the car.*

FIG. 6: *A windflow simulation over a car and rear wing.*

3D PRINTING CHECKLISTS

Before Printing Your CAD

- See 3D Printing Basics on page 9 for printing tips.

- Print the automobile wing.

- After printing, remove any excess material with a file.

Quality Control & Product Testing

- Test the print as indicated in step 6 on page 137.

THINK ABOUT IT

Consider these questions and make notes about possible answers. You can test them by modifying and printing a new version of your design.

How does the wing/spoiler on the back of the car help to keep the car on the road surface at high speeds?

What would happen if you moved the wing to the bottom of the rear bumper?

DESIGN CHALLENGE

Can you design a rearwing for the car that has a curved topface but has a flat bottom face? How do you think this wing will impact the performance of the car?

THE SCIENCE BEHIND IT

Wings are designed so that one side of the wing has a larger surface width than the other. This cause the air to take longer to flow over one side than the other. This causes a pressure difference on either side of the wing, thereby causing lift (in planes) or downforce (in cars). Use of wings in cars became popular through Formula 1 racing, in which cars go at high speed, causing lift, so the wing helps to create downforce that keeps the car grounded.

GLOSSARY

Additive Manufacturing – the process of manufacturing an object by adding material layer by layer based on a pre-defined pattern/design

Autodesk Flow Design – a fluid flow simulation software that lets you insert objects in the path of a flowing fluid and view the impact (disturbance) to the flow.

Ball-and-Socket Joint – a non-rigid joint between two parts (the ball and the socket). The ball inserts into the socket and can rotate freely within the confines of the socket.

CAD—Computer-Aided Design – is a computer-based method of virtually drawing 2D and 3D objects as a step towards designing objects without having to make or manufacture them with the actual material.

Chamfers – a chamfer is a slice cut out of an edge where two faces meet. Both faces of the edge still remain after a chamfer but are reduced in area

Concentric – two circles having the same center and slightly smaller than the other, so that there is an even distance between each circle wall on all sides.

Dovetail Joint – a joint that temporarily connects two objects by interconnecting a dove-shaped tail with a dove-shaped pin.

Ergonomic – a design that is comfortable for humans to operate given our bodies limitations

Extrusion – the process of shaping a raw material by pushing it through a patterned shape

Flush Joint – a joint where two or more pieces merge so their faces are in the same plane with no gaps

Force Meter – a device that measures the force applied to it

Force Sensor – the sensor on the force meter/device that senses the change in force applied

Frets – narrow rises on the neck of a guitar that can be used to modify the vibrating length of a guitar string, thereby varying the sound the string makes when plucked.

Ligaments – organic material/tissue in the human body that attaches bone to other bones.

Mechanical Vise – a devise with two parts/jaws that can be gradually brought closer together to grip an object within the jaws.

Phalanx – the bones in the human finger

Plastic Filament – a material used in 3D printers that is made of plastic

Polylactic Acid (PLA) – this is a type of plastic filament used in 3D printers to create objects

Press fit – a joint between objects with tight tolerances so they can be joined by merely pressing them together

Proximal – closer to the body (the part of the finger closer to the body/palm)

SketchUp – 3D modeling software

SnapGrid – the tool in Tinkercad that lets you adjust the measurements of objects by fixed increments

STL File – a file format used to save 3D designs and use for 3D printing

Tinkercad – 3D modeling software

Workplane – the plane in 3D modeling software on which the designs are built and manipulated

ANSWERS

There are numerous questions placed throughout the book as extension activities for readers. Here are answer to some of them. It is important to note than many questions have multiple correct answers, though some may be more efficient than others. It is best to design and print a few and then test them out.

LAB 1

Is the printed object lighter or heavier than you expected? Why do you think it is so?
Objects that are 3D-printed are lighter or heavier than most people expect based on the infill. The infill is the amount of material filled in between faces/walls of the object. Most 3D printers will let you adjust this from none/minimal infill to completely solid. Since solid objects (with 100% infill) have more infill, they are heavier. The pattern of infill also impacts the strength of the object.

Did you get a chance to see the inside of the object as it was printing? What did it look like?
The inside will typically have a hexagonal pattern, but can vary depending on the setting of your 3D printer. You can also pause the print midway through the process to visually inspect the object.

LAB 2

What do you notice about the curved face of the cylinder (its texture, its "roundness")?
Most printers will approximate a circle to multiple short lines. The corresponding curved face thus may feel like many flat

rectangular faces fit tightly together. You can increase the approximation to more rectangles, which will give a smoother curved surface.

LAB 3

What was the strategy you used to put the puzzle together?
There are various strategies to put the tangram puzzle together to make a square. One way is to draw square and try to fit the pieces inside it. Another might be to start with the two large triangles and then work your way to the rest of the pieces.

Is there any relationship between the pieces? If so, explain.
The small triangle is ½ the area of the square and a ⅓ the area of the large triangle. There are many other relationships that can be identified among the various pieces.

LAB 4

Is there a limitation to the size of a hole in an object? If so, why?
The size of the hole in an object is limited by the walls of the object. Further, if the hole is too close to the wall you risk impacting the stability of the wall. Engineers have strict guidelines for distance of holes based on their size and the material of the object.

Can the hookhole be in a corner of the earring? Why? Or why not?
Sometimes an earring is expected to hang freely with a hook, in such situations you want to have the hookhole furthest away from the center (or the center of gravity). The corners, in our design, fit this require

ment. You can also have the hole closer to the center of the triangle, but this will impact how freely it will hang.

LAB 5

What would happen if the donut slice arc was 0.4 instead of 0.6?
The arc would lead to a hook that was flatter or less curved. This might make it easier for objects hung from the hook to fall/slip off. Too tight an arc might make it hard to hang objects on it. Try different designs and see what works best.

Why should the holes be at least 2mm from the edge?
Holes decrease the strength (structural integrity) of the material around the hole. If we make a hole that is too close to the edge, the screw may crack the hole and the edge. A 2 mm gap between the edge and the hole minimizes this possibility. A larger gap (tolerance) is also advised.

LAB 6

List two different architectural styles that are incorporated in your structures.
There are numerous architectural styles: Classical, Neoclassical, Brutalist, Gothic, Baroque, etc. The architectural styles for your buildings will vary based on the time and location they were built/designed.

Why do you think one architectural style was selected over the other for these structures?
Architectural styles are selected depending on the purpose of the building, the impact

for the desired tenants, cost, architects, style and education, and other factors.

LAB 7

Can you design a handle for the comb for a soldier who has lost his thumb?

The requirement for gripping the comb is contact area between the fingers and the comb, and the ability to sandwich the handle between two parts of the finger. With an opposable thumb, this is easily achieved. However, if a thumb is not available, we can increase the width of the handle so the fingers can curl around it. The handle will now be sandwiched between the tips of the fingers and the palm. Other options might be to create grooves in the handle for the fingers to slip into.

What would happen if the teeth were 3 mm apart instead of 1.5 mm?

A wider gap between the teeth would mean less hair combed per stroke. Also, the hair that does get combed will get chunked instead of being stranded.

LAB 8

Can you design a paperclip that has a wireframe of an animal, bird, or fish? How could you modify the design to make the paperclip less flexible?

Search these options online to see more possible solutions. Decreasing the thickness of the paper clip at the point where it flexes (where the top of the clip attaches to the bottom of the clip) will make it more flexible. Top and bottom are identified as when the paperclip is attached to a paper—being on top of the paper, and at the bottom/behind the paper.

LAB 9

How could you modify the design to make the pasta spoon grab wet pasta better?

A simple solution would be to increase the length of the teeth/prongs of the pasta spoon. Designers can experiment with different angles of the prongs or of the bowl itself. A handle length of 10 inches/25.4 cm or more is usually long enough for deeper pasta pots which will prevent your hand from getting burned. This will in turn give you more time to grab the pasta with a spoon. Also, consider changing the hole in the middle to slotted holes—the water will still drain, but less pasta is likely to slip out.

LAB 10

Modify the letter O to make it more resistant to deformation.

If we square the letter O so that it is less round, it will be more resistant to deformation. Additional options would be to increase the thickness of the letter.

Do any letters return to their original shape after they are taken out of the vise? If so, why?

The letter M is a good example of a letter that deforms and then returns to its original shape after the force is removed. The flexibility of a part of an object is determined by the material and the number of points it is attached (degrees of freedom). The external stems of the letter M are only attached at one point to the rest of the letter, so they have more flexibility than, say, the letter A, whose external stems re connect at one end a and in the middle as well.

LAB 11

Why do we need to slow down the water in the reef?

The polyps in the reef and other small fish (like clownfish) consume plankton from the flowing water. By slowing down the water flow, they have more opportunity to feed on the plankton.

LAB 12

Why is there a pea (sphere) in the whistle?

The pea disrupts the air flow in the whistle, which creates a unique sound that is more effective at getting people's attention. Some whistles do not have peas, or have other modifications to achieve the same effect.

What modification would you make to the design if you wanted to create different sounds from the same whistle?

The sound is created by the air flow over the edge of the hole in the whistle. By modifying the edge or the size of the hole we can vary the amplitude and pitch of the whistle. We can also move the position of the whistle hole to achieve further variation. Try different options out and see what works best.

LAB 13

Why do we need the dimensions of the tail section to be slightly smaller than the socket section?

The tail and socket sections need to slide into each other. This will not be possible if they are the same dimension. Therefore, there should be a difference in dimensions between the two. Engineers have specific guidance on the difference (tolerance) for these dimensions.

LAB 14

Can you modify only one part of the design so the phone holder can hold the phone upright at more than one position?

Set the back rest at an angle with the vertical axis. This way it will stand at two different angles based on which end is dovetailed first.

How does the lip help the design objectives?

The lip keeps the mounted phone from sliding, thereby maintaining its position in the holder.

How did you/could you adapt your design to make it as flat as possible when disassembled?

Determine which part has the greatest thickness when disassembled. Then flatten it proportionally so it maintains its functionality. For example, if the lip is the thickest/highest part, decrease its thickness to 1 mm, enough to keep the phone from sliding.

LAB 15

What would happen if the difference between the diameter of the ball and the internal diameter of the socket were only 0.5 mm apart?

As in the tolerances for the dovetail joint, there should be at least 1 mm difference (tolerance) between the ball and socket so it can rotate freely.

Why are there slots in the socket?

The tolerances between the ball and socket diameters are kept tight so the ball is limited to rotational motion (no sliding/linear motion) in the socket. This means that the widest part of the ball has to pass through a smaller opening at the top of the socket as it is inserted in place. The close tolerances will not permit this. Therefore, we create slots in the side of the socket so it can expand as the ball is inserted, but then return to its original shape after the ball is installed.

LAB 16

Can you lock the camera in the vertical position without a key?

It may be possible to create a system of notches and studs that mate between the ball and socket itself. Though it might be less efficient and harder to 3D print. Explore other possibilities.

What would happen if we made the key seat at the point of the slots in the socket section?

The key seat located at the point of the slots would still lock the joint for some positions, but would permit rotation in a plane parallel to the slot.

LAB 17

Can you use another dovetail joint to lock two puzzle pieces together that are not locked together directly now?

All pieces are connected directly except for the two smaller red pieces. We cannot connect these two without first removing some other joint or modification to the design.

LAB 18

How would using the ball and socket joint designed in Lab 15 change how the finger moves?

The ball and socket joint in Lab 15 allows for equal rotational motion in all directions as well as equal pitch and roll in all directions. The ball and socket joint in this Lab has increased pitch in the direction where there is a shorter wall for the socket.

LAB 19

Can you design the elbow joint to restrict lateral motion so it matches a real human elbow?

Increasing the socket at height in the direction you want to restrict motion will lock motion in that direction (similar to the knuckles joint in Lab 17).

How would using the ball and socket joint designed in Lab 18 for the knuckles change how the shoulder moves?

This would allow for rotational motion of the shoulder, but would limit motion in the plane that has a lower socket wall.

LAB 20

How would you modify the sound hole to increase the volume?

Increasing the perimeter of the sound hole will increase the volume.

Why did we use the New Banana tool instead of a basic shape tool to hollow out the guitar?

A basic shape tool like a cylinder would create a hollowed-out section in the guitar with a large overhang. The New Banana tool allows us to shape the hollow to match the contours of the guitar, but also minimize the overhangs for the ceiling of the hollowed-out part.

LAB 21

What would happen if we swap the positions of the button and lock from Step 5?

The switch would make it harder for the lock to lock and unlock, as well as the taper on the button would make it more likely to slip. Although, if the size and shape were modified, it might not make much of a difference.

LAB 22

What is a Creative Commons License Type?

A Creative Commons license allows for free distribution by an author of otherwise copyrighted work. By using the CC symbol.

LAB 23

What was the procedural difference designing in Tinkercad versus SketchUp?

In Tinkercad we began with a 3D basic shape and manipulated its dimensions to a desired size. In SketchUp we began with a 2D shape and extruded into a desired size.

LAB 24

What happened if you extended the push of the hole past the bottom edge of the cylinder?

Push the hole past the bottom edge of the cylinder results in the creation of a through hole.

LAB 25

Would this menu holder help to keep any length paper upright? Why? Or why not?

The menu holder keeps the paper upright by curving it. This curvature dissipates (decreases) radially outward from the menu holder. For larger sheets of paper, there will be no curvature at the far end from the menu holder. This will allow for it to fold.

LAB 26

How does the wing/spoiler on the back of the car help to keep the car on the road surface at high speeds?

The wing/spoiler causes the air to flow over different distances on the top and the bottom of the wing. This causes a downforce that pushes the car down to the road surface.

What would happen if you moved the wing to the bottom of the rear bumper?

There are many different faces on the bottom of the car that change the flow of air, so it is harder to make an accurate prediction. However, assuming smooth flow till it reaches the bumper, the wing at the bottom would likely cause further downforce. This has been used in a variety of race cars to support during cornering. However, it has been found to be hard to control.

ACKNOWLEDGMENTS

I would like to acknowledge the support of my son Joseph and partner Azish, who encouraged and supported me in creating my STEM nonprofit, which was the parent for this book. I also want to acknowledge designers Michael Parker, Lily Su, and Nelson De Jesus Ubri, who have developed the course and provided valuable feedback and insight into the impact of the lessons on students. I want to thank my editor Joy Aquilino, who encouraged me to write this book, and who has demonstrated extreme patience at my lack of knowledge of the editorial and book marketing process. And finally, the many people in my life: my engineering school mentor Carl Wood, my education mentor Joyce Dixon, and others who have helped me develop my understanding of the various skills that put me in a position to write this book.

ABOUT THE AUTHOR

Eldrid Sequeira is an educator and engineer who has spent almost 20 years in education, first as a teacher, then in education management. He is currently the Director of STEM (Science, Technology, Engineering, and Math) at Public Preparatory Network in New York City, leading the charter school network's focus on constructivist learning in STEM and high growth in academic proficiency. Previously, Sequeira held roles in managing math and technology-based education programs for more than 300 K–12 schools for the New York City Department of Education. He is also the founder of Dimension Learning, an award-winning nonprofit organization that has been providing after-school STEM programming to students in grades 2–12 in New York City for five years. A frequent speaker on STEM education and careers, Sequeira has made appearances at the New York City Mathematics Project Annual Educators Conference, ChickTech NYC ACT-W Conference, and World Maker Faire New York. He is the creative driving force behind the curriculum at Dimension Learning and numerous other STEM programs through the NYC Department of Education and with Public Prep. He lives in New York City.